IMAGES
of America

HUTTO

This February 1984 photograph taken by Donna Fowler looks out at Hugh Davenport Sr. (left) and Mike Fowler, this book's author and Donna's husband, from inside their house. Mike cut an opening in the west side of his home to add a fireplace, and Hugh Davenport Sr., his neighbor across the street, had come by to check out the progress. Mike had earlier asked Hugh to begin to record the history of Hutto, and by 1983, Hugh had recorded well over 500 pages of Hutto's history in a very limited photocopy publication titled *An Album of Facts (and Some Contradiction) In Words and Pictures Concerning the History of Hutto.* It is probable that without the past work of Hugh Davenport Sr., Fowler would not have undertaken this project with Arcadia Publishing.

On the Cover: In this 1902 photograph taken from the northeast corner of Farley Street on a busy shopping day in Hutto, people, horses, carriages, and wagons fill East Street. Hutto was a vibrant boom town at the time of this photograph. Industrious Swedish immigrants had flooded into the Hutto area by then were the largest ethnic group in Hutto. The activity in this photograph is only part of the picture: the not-pictured alley on the west side of the buildings to the right is where many of the horses and wagons were hitched to allow for entrance through the doors facing the alley. (Courtesy Holman family collection.)

IMAGES
of America

HUTTO

Mike Fowler

ARCADIA
PUBLISHING

Published by Arcadia Publishing
Charleston SC, Chicago IL, Portsmouth NH, San Francisco CA

Library of Congress Control Number: 2009928332

For all general information contact Arcadia Publishing at:
Telephone 843-853-2070
Fax 843-853-0044
E-mail sales@arcadiapublishing.com
For customer service and orders:
Toll-Free 1-888-313-2665

Visit us on the Internet at www.arcadiapublishing.com

This book is dedicated to my loving wife, Donna Fowler.

CONTENTS

ACKNOWLEDGMENTS

Special thanks are extended to Skip Davenport, Charlie and Clarice Hanstrom, the Holman family, the Hutto Chamber of Commerce, the Hutto Economic Development Corporation, the Aguilar family, Ed and Julia Schmidt, Greg Farley, Earl Klattenhoff, Buddy Holmstrom, the Kerley family, Iola Sturm, the Cage family, Margaret Crislip, Emelia Johnson, the Madrid family, Larry Rydell, Lois Stern, Jesse Rios, Isaac "Jock" Norman, the Vic Stern family, the Oman family, Jim and Carol Wilson, Ron Whitfield, the writings of amateur historians, the many local newspaper publications, the writings of Harvey Olander, *Hutto and Hippos* by Betty Sue Blackman Holmstrom, the writings of Lois Gainer, and anyone else who helped with this endeavor. Great appreciation is also expressed to the many other individuals and families who assisted in bringing this part of Hutto's history back for all to enjoy. Thanks to all of those who honor our past.

INTRODUCTION

Before there ever was a Hutto, there was the land, the flora and fauna, and the Native Americans, primarily the Tonkawa tribe. Prior to Hutto being settled, the first two stores in Williamson County were located on Brushy Creek in the Shiloh and Rice's Crossing communities, just southeast of present-day Hutto. Many of Hutto's early settlers came from those areas.

In 1854, a slave, Adam Orgain, was the first settler in the immediate Hutto vicinity and had been placed out on the black land prairie to watch over his owners' property. Hutto, Texas, was not really established until 1876, when the International and Great Northern Railroad passed through land owned by James Emory Hutto. The fledgling railroad town was named for him, and in 1877, he served as its first postmaster. The railroad officials designated the stop "Hutto Station," and the town of Hutto was born. James E. Hutto came to Texas in 1847 and moved his family into Williamson County in 1855. It was in 1876 that Hutto sold 50 acres to the Texas Land Company of New York for a town site and railroad right-of-way.

Other early settlers in the area were the Carpenter, Davis, Evans, Farley, Goodwin, Highsmith, Johnson, Magle, Payne, Saul, Weight, Womack, and Wright families. Other people living in Hutto during the 1890s included the Dahlberg, Flinn, Hanstrom, M. B. Kennedy, Hugh Kimbro, William McCutcheon, Green Randolph, J. B. Ross, Tinning, and Tisdale families. Soon a great many more people, primarily Swedish and German immigrants with their own language and culture, came to this area to farm and ranch and begin their new lives in America. A railroad depot was built in 1877 with W. H. Farley Sr. as the first railroad agent, and the business area of Hutto was originally located on the south side of the railroad tracks. When Farley retired, he was succeeded by his son, W. H. Farley Jr. In 1900, Mrs. W. H. Farley Jr. (Ava) was successful in securing funds to build a new depot, which served Hutto until it burned down in 1945. A new 1945 depot was built and has since been removed. The first store owner for the south side business center was a Mr. Lloyd, followed by Davis, Blanton, Hudson, Robinson, and others who built various kinds of stores. Sam Monday operated Hutto's first saloon, and a Mr. Scott later owned a similar business. On June 19, 1886, a severe storm hit the small town and wiped out the south side business district, including the first Hutto School, built in 1882, and the Fist Baptist Church of Hutto, built in 1883. In 1890, a vibrant rebuilding effort took place, this time on the north side of the railroad tracks, and by 1892, two rows of store buildings surrounded East Street, the new main street of downtown Hutto. During the early 1890s, Hutto prospered and grew because of the fertile black land soil opportunities that permitted tremendous cotton production on the surrounding farms and spurred the establishment of numerous cotton gins. Community activity abounded with the railroad for transporting goods and can-do spirit of the settlers and immigrants. The soil in the Hutto vicinity was described as "mainly a deep, dark hog-wallow" that grew excellent crops. One of the earliest gins was owned by a Mr. Brown and a Mr. Aten about 1890; a Mr. Cato owned another gin, John R. Hutto and John Flinn owned a gin together, Charles Hanstrom was a partner in a gin, and a Mr. Holman and a Mr. Short built their cotton gin soon after these other gins were established. Saturdays were an extremely active time in downtown Hutto with people and horse-drawn vehicles everywhere. The comment was made by an observant citizen that "No one had better get in a hurry in Hutto on a Saturday because you just couldn't move fast through all the crowd in town." It was reported that one merchant once took in $5,000 on a Saturday in his Hutto store.

By 1898, thanks to the industry of its people and its strong agricultural base, the town of Hutto was bustling and had grown to support six churches, one school, one photography gallery, one confectionery store, one hotel, two drugstores, seven dry good stores, one bank, one tailor shop, one shoe shop, four blacksmiths, eight grocery stores including one meat market, one livery stable, one millinery shop, one lumber yard, one newspaper, two hardware stores, two cotton gins, one gristmill, and five doctors. The first bank was a private institution owned by William M. Woolsey and A. W. Carpenter. It was later bought by E. P. Wilborn and became the Farmers and Merchants State Bank. Later the Hutto National Bank was established, and the Hutto community had two banks. Harry Mauritz was a banker at this time. Early business enterprises were Hutto Hardware, owned by J. T. McCutcheon and W. E. Chapman; Oatts and Christian Hardware; the Jim Holman, Will May, and Carl Hanson furniture store; Bland and Will Harrison dry goods and grocery store; Will Tompkins and Frank Dahlberg's general merchandise store; J. P. Saul Sr.'s general store; and Niels Larsen's blacksmith shop. The doctors in Hutto in the 1890s included Drs. Percy, Harper, A. Nowlin, Howze, and McCowan. An earlier practitioner in Hutto had been Dr. John Carroll Flinn, whose son, Dr. Frank Joe Flinn, also practiced medicine in Hutto. There was also a dentist in the 1890s named George Bruce. In 1902, a fire destroyed almost all of the east side businesses on East Street in downtown when a gasoline stove exploded in the Jackson Restaurant.

Later in Hutto history, there were interesting enterprises such as the Good Luck Potato Chip Company, a funeral parlor, the Hutto Bottling Company, an outdoor theater—the Hippodrome—and a variety of both everyday and unusual businesses.

On July 17, 1911, the town was officially incorporated, and W. D. Holman served as the first mayor of the city of Hutto. Charles E. Hanstrom Sr. played an extremely vital role in the development of early Hutto. The town might not have incorporated had Hanstrom, along with J. D. Tinning, not installed the Hanstrom and Tinning Water Works in 1910 through his purchase of a drilling rig, with which he drilled the first deepwater well in the town. This was a phenomenal year for Charles Hanstrom, for in 1910, he also built the first power plant for Hutto, installing wires and poles and placing wiring in homes; additionally, he started the first ice factory for the community and also partnered with Tinning in a cotton gin. It was this same James D. Tinning who had invented a better cotton planter in 1897, for which he received patent No. 591,613 from the U.S. Patent Office.

In spite of the First World War, the city of Hutto and the surrounding community had a bright future. Cotton was still king—until 1929 and the collapse of the stock market. A long, hard Depression had begun. The two banks at that time, Farmers and Merchants State Bank and Hutto National Bank, both closed during the Great Depression, as did most of the other businesses in the city. Hutto, as a town and community, never fully recovered from this and struggled to the outbreak of and through World War II. Following World War II, a new optimism took over in Hutto, and the community has continually progressed. More recent history has resulted in positive changes for the Hutto community too numerous to recount in this book. In the 1990s, the city of Hutto doubled in size from 630 people in 1990 to 1,250 people in 2000. In 2009, the population of the Hutto has grown to approximately 18,000 residents. Hutto has been truly blessed with our history and the many opportunities that await our community.

One

PEOPLE MAKE HUTTO

This is an early-1900s photograph of James Emory Hutto, for whom the Hutto community is named. Born in South Carolina, he lived in Alabama and arrived in Texas on January 16, 1847, and settled at Webber's Prairie near Austin. James Emory Hutto married Margaret Hughes on September 6, 1849, and eventually had six sons and three daughters. He helped George Glasscock build the first gristmill in Georgetown. In 1854, Hutto moved to the area north of Brushy Creek in Williamson County that would be named for him when the railroad came through his land. Hutto was appointed the first postmaster in Hutto on June 27, 1877. (Courtesy Hugh S. Davenport Sr. Collection.)

A late-1880s photograph shows Thomas "Tom" Abraham Evans and his wife, Fanny Ellen (McCutcheon) Evans, dressed for their portrait. The Evans family was among the earliest settlers of Hutto. They had 15 children, all born in Williamson County. Tom and Fanny are buried side by side in the Shiloh-McCutcheon Cemetery southeast of Hutto. (Courtesy Margaret Crislip Collection.)

The Jessie A. McCutcheon and Elizabeth Jane (Harrell) McCutcheon two-story home in Hutto with Elizabeth and four of her 13 children are pictured. The McCutcheon family was among the earliest settlers of Hutto. (Courtesy Margaret Crislip Collection.)

Dr. John Carroll Flinn was born in Tennessee in 1829. In January 1870, he came to Texas with his wife, Susan Frances (McGuire) Flinn, and soon bought land in the Shiloh area southeast of Hutto, where he raised cattle and cotton. They had 16 children, of whom 13 reached adulthood. One son, Dr. Joe Frank Flinn, practiced medicine for over a quarter of a century in Hutto until his death in 1929. (Courtesy Thomas H. Flinn III Collection.)

James Dommel, an early German settler of the Hutto area, is pictured in this tintype photograph. A tintype photograph was made by creating a direct positive image on a sheet of metal that was painted, lacquered, or enameled to create a blackened background surface. (Courtesy Hugh S. Davenport Sr. Collection.)

Thomas Henry Flinn was born in Bolivar, Tennessee, as the Civil War ended in 1865. Thomas was a very active participant in Hutto and in Williamson County. Thomas Flinn was one of seven sons of Dr. John Carroll and Susan (McGuire) Flinn. He married Eldora Mae (Kimmons) on July 8, 1894, in Hutto; they had four children, all born in Hutto. Flinn served as postmaster of Hutto from 1893 to 1897 and as Williamson County clerk from 1904 until 1912. He was also an early mayor of the city of Hutto from 1920 to 1922. Thomas was a teacher, ran a newspaper—the *Hutto Enterprise*—was a printer, and was a part owner of a Hutto drugstore with one of his brothers, George. (Courtesy Hugh S. Davenport Sr. Collection.)

William Henry Farley Sr. was the first Hutto Depot agent in Hutto from 1877 to 1896. He was born in July 1828 in Alabama to John Thompson Farley and Mary Ann (Allen) Farley. After the Civil War, in about 1870, it is documented that Mary Ann Farley brought her two sons, William Henry Farley (later known as "Sr.") and Fredrick Forest Farley (later known as "Uncle Fed"), with her to Hutto. William H. Farley Sr. had married Lucy Ann (Hargrove) Farley in Alabama, and they had five sons, most born in Texas. (Courtesy Hugh S. Davenport Sr. Collection.)

This photograph of William H. Farley Sr. and his wife, Lucy A. (Hargrove) Farley, was taken by local photographer Ramsey of Hutto, Texas. William H. Farley Sr. and Jr. were well-respected business, civic, and religious leaders in the town of Hutto. William H. Farley Sr. died on August 20, 1909, and is buried in the Shiloh Cemetery near Hutto. (Courtesy Hugh S. Davenport Sr. Collection.)

Ramsey,   HUTTO, TEXAS.

H. A. Highsmith was born on January 11, 1843, and died on March 19, 1930. He was a Civil War veteran, a Texas Ranger, and part of the posse that helped capture outlaw Sam Bass. On July 31, 1867, Highsmith married Sarah A. McCutcheon, and they remained married for almost 63 years, living their last 45 years in Hutto. Sarah was born on January 14, 1844, and died March 2, 1930. (Courtesy Hugh S. Davenport Sr. Collection.)

13

Edward Rogan and his brother William came to Hutto from Scotland. Edward married Hannah Blackstock, and they had two children, Joseph Rogan and Barbara Rogan. Barbara Rogan married Walter Martin, and they had two sons, Cecil and Raymond, and a daughter also named Barbara. Notice in the photograph of Edward Rogan with his rifle the hitching posts in front of his homestead. (Courtesy Hugh S. Davenport Sr. Collection.)

This early-1900s studio photograph shows, from left to right, George Martin, Bill Goodwin, Alex Martin, and Will Glendenning dressed for the occasion. Alex and George Martin were brothers and served in World War I along with another brother, Jack. Their parents were Peter Martin and Jemina (Glendenning) Martin. Will Glendenning was Jemina's brother. Bill (or Will) Goodwin never married. (Courtesy Margaret Crislip Collection.)

This *c.* 1902 photograph of Hutto includes the well-dressed music pupils taught by Miss Powell. From left to right are (first row) Bertha Brooks (Thompson), Lilian Hutto (A. Townes), Mary Metcalf (R. Woodward), unidentified, Ottie Harris, and Esther Matthews (Bird); (second row) Effie Brooks (V. Harris), unidentified, Miss Powell, Jennie Davis, Annie Norman (Patterson), and Irene Norman; (third row) Lucy Goodwin (Koger), Nean Harris (A. Farley), Maud Harris (W. Farley), Huldah Goodwin (Davenport), unidentified, and Annie Short. (Courtesy Hugh S. Davenport Sr. Collection.)

This Ramsey of Hutto studio photograph shows two young men, Oliver Bird (left) and Alvin Walling (right), in the early 1900s. (Courtesy Hugh S. Davenport Sr. Collection.)

Ramsey.   HUTTO, TEXAS.

15

Photographed from top down are four generations of the Hutto family: James Emery Hutto Sr., John Riley Hutto (son), William Travis Hutto (grandson), and William Burnice Hutto (great-grandson). James Emery Hutto was born in Greenville, South Carolina, on May 8, 1824, came via Alabama to Texas (Webber's Prairie near Austin) in January 1847, and settled in what became Hutto in 1854. (Courtesy Hugh S. Davenport Sr. Collection.)

Ten early Hutto adult band members pose with their instruments. All of the band members are wearing hats. Notice the ladies in the background. Bert Payne, second from the right, was a trumpet player, and John Spong was also a member of this band. (Courtesy Buddy Holmstrom Collection.)

Early babies of Hutto are sitting on a decorative rug on the porch. Pictured from left to right are John Testmann, Clara May Stockard, unidentified with cat, Dorothy Burns, Edith Harrison, Donald Campbell, and Emiel Smith. The adults are unidentified. Note the foundation of cedar posts and the shiplap siding on the house, typical construction in Hutto in the early days. (Courtesy Buddy Holmstrom Collection.)

Mr. and Mrs. James B. Gainer of Hutto are pictured at their home. James B. Gainer was born in 1855 and died in 1945. The Gainers were the parents of Lonnie O. Gainer, born December 19, 1880, and Herbert E. Gainer, born December 13, 1885. Note the hand saw hanging from a nail on the board-and-batten siding of the structure. (Courtesy Hugh S. Davenport Sr. Collection from Lois Gainer.)

Eleven of the Hutto women are posed on a board sidewalk with a wagon in the background at the old Hutto family homestead. (Courtesy Hugh S. Davenport Sr. Collection.)

Ten of the Hutto men stand on a board sidewalk with the old homestead in the background. James Emory Hutto Sr. is on the extreme left. (Courtesy Hugh S. Davenport Sr. Collection.)

One of the first automobiles in Hutto, around 1905, belonged to Dr. John D. Porter, M.D. Also in the vehicle are Philip Davenport and his son, Hugh S. Davenport. (Courtesy Hugh S. Davenport Sr. Collection.)

This 1907 photograph shows Mary Allen (Farley) Goodwin, Hugh Goodwin, and their second son, William F. "Bill" Goodwin, posed with their dog and horse (a mare named Maude used by Mary as a buggy horse for many years) in front of their beautiful Victorian home located just west of the old city limits of Hutto. Hugh Goodwin came to Hutto in 1877 and purchased more than 400 acres next to land owned by James Emory Hutto Sr. The home pictured above was severely damaged by a tornado on May 1, 1944, and was torn down for the salvage value. (Courtesy Hugh S. Davenport Sr. Collection.)

Dave "Tamer" Barnes of Hutto is pictured in his derby hat, tie, three-piece suit, and boots. (Courtesy Hugh S. Davenport Sr. Collection from Lucy Barnes.)

Hilda Serafia Sylvan, wife of Pastor O. H. Sylvan, the first full-time pastor of Hutto Lutheran Church, is seen in their parsonage home. In 1899, they came to Hutto, where he pastored for the next 14 years and four months until 1914. This home was the first parsonage of their church. Through the door in this picture is the dining room, where the Swedish-born Pastor Sylvan and other area Lutheran pastors planned the creation of Trinity College of Round Rock, founded in 1906. Serafia died in their home on May 13, 1913, and is buried at Hutto Lutheran Cemetery. (Author's collection.)

Henry Albert Highsmith is pictured in his later years in Hutto holding the reins to his horse and buggy with 16-spoke wheels. In the background are a four-pronged pitchfork and a cotton field. Highsmith was famous for his help with the capture of the outlaw Sam Bass. H. A. Highsmith was born in Bastrop, Texas, on January 11, 1843. In 1878, H. A. helped take the mortally wounded robber Sam Bass into custody after a failed bank robbery and back into Round Rock. Highsmith and others guarded Sam Bass in the Hart Hotel until Bass died. Henry Albert's cousin, Williamson County deputy sheriff Ahijah W. Grimes, was shot six times and killed by the Bass gang in that robbery attempt. In 1885, Highsmith moved to Hutto, where he lived until his death on March 19, 1930. (Courtesy Hugh S. Davenport Sr. Collection.)

This early photograph of four horsemen of Hutto includes, from left to right, Will (or Bill) Goodwin (died unmarried), Bill Bowden (ran the telephone company in Hutto), Spencer Goodwin (married Alice Evans and had two daughters, Katherine Goodwin Cosby and Louise Goodwin Tate), and Roy Holman. (Courtesy Hugh S. Davenport Sr. Collection.)

Of these people on the International and Great Northern Railroad (I&GNRR) tracks and trestles in Hutto, only two are identified: on the back right are Edwin Farley and Pearl Norman. The large structure on the left is the Round Bale Gin, a longtime landmark in Hutto's past. Behind Farley to the right is the railroad handcar housing. In 1876, the railroad came to Hutto, and on December 28, 1876, it had reached Austin. The International and Great Northern Railroad Company later became a major part of the Missouri Pacific lines in Texas. (Courtesy Hugh S. Davenport Sr. Collection.)

These young ladies are from well-known Hutto families. Pictured from left to right are Ollie Inez Nelson (Hutto High School class of 1915), Mae Brown (class of 1915), Martha Segred Gustafson (class of 1915), Lillian Busch, Margaret Bowden (class of 1913), Mary Esther Highsmith (class of 1915), and Ida Matthews (class of 1917). (Courtesy Hugh S. Davenport Sr. Collection.)

In 1916, almost the entire congregation of Hutto Lutheran Church was photographed in front of the second and newly completed two-story parsonage. The parsonage initially served for more than a decade as the residence for Pastor C. J. Rosenquist and his family. Pastor Rosenquist was from Sweden and served the Hutto Lutheran Church from 1915 to 1928. In 1951, this structure with wraparound porches on both floors was torn down, and much of the lumber was used for the third parsonage. (Courtesy Larry Rydell.)

These two World War I soldiers from Hutto posing by the barracks are Homer Hardwick (left) and Lawrence H. Miller (right) of Company H, 2nd Texas Infantry, U.S. Army. The soldiers peering from the wood and canvas-covered barracks are unidentified. This photograph was taken on May 20, 1917. It is known that at least two soldiers from Hutto died in World War I: Cpl. Lawrence H. Miller (pictured) and Pvt. Henry Miller. Lawrence H. Miller was with 141st Infantry Regiment, 36th Division in France when he died on October 8, 1918, and is buried at Plot H, Row 17, Grave 9 in the Meuse-Argonne American Cemetery in Romagne, France. He was posthumously awarded the French Croix de Guerre. (Courtesy Buddy Holmstrom Collection.)

Buddy Robinson of Hutto was one of many who served in the U.S. Army during World War I. (Courtesy Hugh S. Davenport Sr. Collection.)

This World War I photograph was taken in 1917 of locals waiting for their Hutto inductees to come to the Hutto Depot from Taylor on their way to their induction in San Antonio. Observe the depot, automobiles, and train cars in front of and on the spur north of the main tracks. The Hutto Depot pictured above was built in 1900. (Courtesy Hugh S. Davenport Sr. Collection.)

This is a World War I–era photograph of U.S. soldier Edmund Johnson with a cane in his right hand; W. H. Farley Jr., the Hutto railroad depot agent, looking up; and Angel Matthews taking aim into the sky with a rifle. (Courtesy Hugh S. Davenport Sr. Collection.)

The six young men of Hutto posed for this c. 1918 photograph are, from left to right, Jim Cooper, Jack Blackman (who later owned Blackman's Garage in Hutto and died in December 1960 while serving as mayor of the city of Hutto), "Coot" Cooper, Emery "Dutch" Blackman (later a charter member of Hutto Lions Club), Glen Blackman, and Cecil Ray. (Courtesy Hugh S. Davenport Sr. Collection.)

Here is a 1950 photograph of another generation of one of the many Swedish Johnson families of Hutto. The Eric Seder "E. S." and Mary Anna Johnson family had four sons and three daughters. From left to right are Kenneth, who was involved in farming and Hutto Co-op activities; Gladys (Hugland); Kermit, who was in farming and worked for Alcoa; Irene (Rydell); Edmund, involved in farming; Alyce (Holmstrom); and Vincent, an army captain in the Korean War and also involved in farming and the Agricultural Stabilization and Conservation Service. The daughters were all homemakers. (Courtesy Buddy Holmstrom Collection.)

The Hutto girls' basketball team won the Williamson County Basketball Championship. Team members pictured with their leather basketball are, from left to right, Mabel Ray (side center, class of 1921), Ester Gustafson (forward), Lucy Brown (team captain and forward, class of 1920), Alta Parsley (coach), Bessie Eugenia Gainer (guard, class of 1923), Elsie Blackman (guard), and Francis Payne (jump center, class of 1921). (Courtesy Buddy Holmstrom Collection.)

This late-1920s photograph of sisters Katherine (left) and Louise Goodwin was taken by the wood fence supported by cedar posts on property across the street from the 402 East Street home currently owned by Margie Schuyler and her husband, Carl Nelson, in the background. A note on back of the photograph states, "This is your Valentine says Louise." (Courtesy Hugh S. Davenport Sr. Collection.)

Thirty-six young ladies who were members of the 1925 Hutto Choral Club were under the direction of Mrs. E. J. Wood in this photograph. Wood is pictured in the top row center dressed in black. (Courtesy Hugh S. Davenport Sr. Collection.)

In this c. 1929 photograph of the Wegstrom and Lidell families, from left to right are (first row) Myrtle Violette Linnea Lidell and Carl Everett Lidell; (second row) Anna Vivette Lidell; Mabel Alda Linnea Wegstrom; Anna Christina (Anderson) Wegstrom and her husband, Carl John Wegstrom, holding Catherine Annette Lidell; and Per Reinhold Lidell and his wife, Myrtle Marie Ingeborg (Wegstrom) Lidell. They are pictured at the Wegstrom home, still located at 108 West Live Oak Street in Hutto. (Author's collection.)

Carl Frithiof "Fritz" Jarnquist was the son of a Swedish blacksmith, Carl Anderson. Fritz immigrated to America at age 15 and came to Texas to make his life as a farmer. In 1911, Fritz married Frida Spong, and they settled in the Hutto area, becoming members of Hutto Evangelical Lutheran Church. The first park of the city of Hutto was named Fritz Park in his honor. (Photograph by Mel Fowler; courtesy Janet Davenport.)

In the 1930s, Pastor R. V. Samuelson and the Ladies Aid Society of Hutto Lutheran Church are pictured as follows: from left to right, (first row) Mrs. Oscar (Bessie) Rehn, Mrs. Albert (Irene) Johnson, Mrs. Alvin (Esther) Johnson, Mrs. Per Reinhold (Myrtle) Lidell, Rev. R. V. Samuelson, Mrs. Robert (Maude) Johnson, Mrs. A. G. Almquist, Mrs. Henry (Stella) Johnson, and Mrs. Albert Peterson; (second row) Mrs. Carl Peterson, Mrs. Anton (Ida) Johnson, Mrs. Carl A. Johnson, unidentified, Mrs. Albert (Signe) Johnson, Mrs. Adolph Johnson, unidentified, Mrs. John Swenson, and Mrs. C. E. Rydell; (third row) Mrs. Will Larson, Mrs. Robert Stromberg, Mrs. J. Emil (Hilda) Johnson, ? Swenson, Mrs. Carl Johan (Anna) Wegstrom, Mrs. Will Spong, Mrs. E. S. (Mary) Johnson, unidentified, Mrs. Arthur Carlson, Mrs. C. O. (Selma) Johnson, Mrs. Werner Swenson, ? Spong, Mrs. Oscar Holmstrom, unidentified, Mrs. Gunnar Chellstrom, Mrs. Ernest E. (Rosa Lee) Johnson, unidentified, Mrs. Oscar Dahl, Mrs. Lambert Johnson, and Mrs. Lambert Johnson. (Courtesy Larry Rydell.)

J. P. Saul Jr. and his family are properly dressed for this early Ramsey of Hutto, Texas, studio photograph. Pictured from left to right are J. P. "Ped" Saul, son Owen, daughter Tona, son Emzy, daughter Woodie, and Ped's wife, Mary Catherine "Callie" (Miller) Saul. The Saul family were some of the earliest settlers of Williamson County, living southeast of Hutto on Brushy Creek. The early Saul men were involved in some of the first cattle drives up the Chisholm Trail. (Courtesy Buddy Holmstrom Collection.)

Ramsey,   HUTTO, TEXAS.

Jack Martin of Hutto served the United States in World War I. Notice the high-laced boots and leather leggings that he wore with his wool uniform in this 1917 photograph. After the war, Jack, who was of Scottish descent, lived and farmed for many years in the Hutto area before his death. (Courtesy Margaret Crislip Collection.)

This E. S. Johnson family photograph was used in the 1918 *Swedes in Texas in Words and Pictures*. Eric S. Johnson of Hutto married Mary Spong in 1905. Pictured by year of birth with them are their children, Irene (1906), Alice (1907), Gladys (1910), Edmund (1914), and Vinson (1917). E. S. was a well-respected farmer in the Hutto community and a deacon at the Hutto Lutheran Swedish Church. (Courtesy Buddy Holmstrom Collection.)

An early-1930s photograph shows the children of Charles and Lydia Stern, a family of German heritage that lived on a farm west of Hutto. Pictured from left to right are Carl Stern, born in 1922; Elvira "Rusty" Stern (Hooper), born in 1929; and Victor Henry Stern, born in 1927. (Courtesy Lois Stern Collection.)

Sam Fisher was a well-respected general handyman in the Hutto community. It is said that he was also an excellent bird hunter, fisherman, and camp cook. According to Charles Hanstrom Jr., "Sam worked at Hanstrom and Tinning for many years." (Courtesy Hugh S. Davenport Sr. Collection.)

Included in this 1930s Holman family portrait, from left to right, are (first row) Isham Lister, H. M. Lister, George Cook Jr., Joe Bill Lister, Willis D. Holman and wife Polly Annis (Lister) Holman, Annabel Holman, and Jim Higgins Holman; (second row) Grace Lister Fowler, Pessell Fowler, Alta Holman, Martin Lister and wife, and George Cook and Bess Lister Cook. Both Willis D. Holman (the first mayor of Hutto in 1911) and his son Jim Higgins Holman served as mayor of Hutto. (Courtesy Holman family collection.)

Two early families of Hutto—Mr. and Mrs. Ed Menielle (left) and Mr. and Mrs. Ira Bird—sit posed for a photograph on the porch. (Courtesy Hugh S. Davenport Sr. Collection.)

Mr. and Mrs. Quirno Moreno lived in Hutto for many years and were devout Catholics who adopted three children: Joseph Moreno, Lidia Moreno Madrid, and Thesesa Cerevantes. Quirno Moreno was born in Rome, Texas, in 1896; as a young man, he rode with Pancho Villa and eventually worked for many years for the Texas Highway Department. Josepha, his wife, was born in Elgin, Texas, in 1904 and was a homemaker. (Courtesy Madrid family collection.)

This is the Future Farmers of America (FFA) Orchestra of Hutto in 1937–1938. The National FFA was founded in 1928. Pictured from left to right are Ernest Johnson, Wesley Brunken with fiddle, Dean Robbins, Hershel Sands, Milton Burrow with guitar, Neal Sorenson with fiddle, and Sam Blackman. (Courtesy Hugh S. Davenport Sr. Collection from Louise Goodwin.)

A bunch of Swedish kids from Hutto and Jonah are shown on the banks of the San Gabriel River around 1939. From left to right are Annette Lidell, Donna Lindgren, Rod Johnson, Gloria Spong, Kenneth Johnson, Gordon Spong, Larry Rydell, Kermit Johnson, Donald Rydell, David Holmstrom, Carroll Holmstrom, and Buddy Holmstrom. (Courtesy Rod Johnson Collection.)

Sam Gainer lived in Hutto and served for 17 years as city marshal. His wife, Lois Gainer, wrote, "There was no regular salary, just a percentage of any fines collected and the City paid for his phone bill. He furnished his own car and many times I drove for him." She worked as cafeteria manager for the Hutto School and later wrote several books, including *Lois Gainer Remembers: 80 Years of Small Town and Country Life in and around Hutto, Texas*. (Author's collection as provided by Lois Gainer.)

Bill Henley is pictured at the Henley Cafe in Hutto, located on the corner of East Street and what is now U.S. Highway 79. This popular store had good food, confectioneries, and often homemade potato chips that Bill and his sister, Riley Henley, made and distributed in the area. In 1923, the store burned, and the cook was killed as a result of the fire. (Courtesy Hutto Chamber of Commerce Collection.)

This mid-1960s photograph shows German heritage farmer Ernest Schneider of Hutto with two of his grandchildren, Don Sturm (left) and Scott Kelm (right), on the family farm that is now completely covered over by State Highway 130. (Courtesy Sturm family collection.)

Three generations of the Rios family have worked in Hutto. *Rios* means "rivers" in Spanish. The photograph on the right is from the 1940 immigration papers of Juan C. Rios where he was listed as an *obrero*, or worker; he worked for John "Poagie" Glendenning for many years. The picture directly below is of Jose B. Rios Sr., who worked at the Hutto Co-op for many years. Their grandson and son respectively, Jesse Rios, pictured below right, worked for the Hutto Co-op for over 17 years and served as a councilman with the City of Hutto for five years. (All courtesy Rios family collection.)

The Jim Cage Sr. and Emma Kellough family had 12 children, nine of whom lived to adulthood. Pictured around 1990, from left to right, are (seated) Willie Mae Barnes, Jim Cage Sr., Emma Kellough, and Jim Cage Jr.; (standing) Cassandra Kitchen, Wilbert Cage, Joyce Spencer, Rita Thomas, Rosetta Cage, Cheryl Jackson, and Charlotte Kerley. All of the children graduated from Hutto High School. (Courtesy Emma Kellough Collection.)

Edmund G. "Ed" Schmidt has legendary status in the Hutto community. He served the City of Hutto in elective capacity as councilman for nine years and another 20 years as mayor from 1970 to 1990. A charter member of the Lions Club, Ed has maintained perfect attendance for over 55 years. He and his wife, Julia, had four children: Dennis, Jennifer, David, and Corliss. (Author's collection.)

The Kerley family of Hutto, pictured around 1979 from left to right, are Allen, Harold Jr., Bernice, Odell, Willie, Emma Kerley, Harold Kerley Sr., Donald, and Ray. Not pictured are Levon, Larry, and Leroy. The Kerleys had nine sons and one daughter. (Courtesy the Kerley family.)

Pictured in 1984 is the family of Marvin Sturm, born May 13, 1933, who married Iola (Schneider) of Hutto on October 24, 1959, and had three children. Marvin served on the Hutto City Council for 14 years. All three children—from left to right, Tammy Gay Sturm (born 1961), Don Marvin Sturm (born 1962), and Mike Gene Sturm (born 1965)—graduated from Hutto High School. Marvin died on July 1, 2001. (Courtesy Sturm family collection.)

Curtis Peterson is of Swedish heritage and a lifelong resident of Hutto who lived in his family home. Much about his home is unchanged from the early 1900s. He appeared in an award-winning movie, *The Unforeseen*, along with other local Hutto residents. The documentary movie with Robert Redford addressed changes resulting from growth in the Central Texas area. (Author's collection.)

Lidia (Moreno) Madrid Gomez was a single mother who worked for the Hutto Independent School District in the Special Education Department and also as a Hutto election polls translator. Pictured about 1975, she and her eight children are, from left to right, (first row) Chris Madrid, Felix Madrid (currently works for the Hutto Independent School District and is a Hutto City councilman), Michelle (Madrid) Selman, and Lidia; (second row) Marcia (Madrid) Brandt, Nick Madrid, Marse Madrid, Michael Madrid, and Cindy (Madrid) Sleppy. (Courtesy Madrid family collection.)

Cpl. Richard Arlen Oman, U.S. Army (Hutto High School class of 1961 and Texas A&M University class of 1965) poses in combat gear with his 5.56-millimeter M16 rifle. Richard was a teacher when he was drafted to serve his country. Richard was born on November 4, 1942, and was killed in action in South Vietnam during the Vietnam War on April 27, 1969. (Courtesy David "Red" Oman Collection.)

This photograph of Emma and Harold Kerley Sr. was taken in 2000. Emma (Sorrel) Kerley was born in 1936. Harold Kerley Sr. was born in 1934 and worked for the Hutto Co-op for 38 years. Harold Kerley Sr. was the grandson of Benjamin "Doc" Kerley, who was the superintendent and teacher at the Hutto Colored School in the early 1900s. (Courtesy the Kerley family.)

This 1975 photograph is of, from left to right, Delores, Rose, Lupe, and Erlinda Aguilar baling and hauling hay in the Hutto area. Their father, Mario Aguilar, owned Aguilar Hauling and worked for many years in dairy farming and agricultural services in the Hutto community. Notice the Cherokee Bale Loader in the picture—Mario Aguilar ordered that piece of equipment and assembled it upon arrival. Rose Aguilar McMillin was the first Mexican American elected to serve on the Hutto City Council. (Courtesy Mario and Mary Ann Aguilar Collection.)

Two

Understanding
Our Past

An 1892 photograph shows early businesses north of the railroad tracks. In the far left background is the east door of a hotel across from the train depot. The Hutto Bank was still unincorporated in 1892. It is during this time that development in Hutto shifted from the south side of the railroad tracks to the north side, creating a new town center on East Street. These two buildings have the same basic exterior look today as they had over a century ago. Note that other buildings on the west side of East Street were not yet constructed. (Courtesy Hugh S. Davenport Sr. Collection.)

The I&GNRR depot in Hutto has a waiting crowd as the steam locomotive comes from Taylor, to the east of Hutto. The Hutto depot sign also has an indicator sign of 261.6 miles to Laredo for those going to the valley. (Courtesy Hutto Chamber of Commerce Collection.)

This early photograph was taken of the International and Great Northern Railroad steam locomotive No. 29 in front of the Hutto Depot and Norman Hotel. On September 30, 1873, the International and Great Northern Railroad Company was created by consolidation of the International Railroad Company and the Houston and Great Northern Railroad. (Courtesy Hugh S. Davenport Sr. Collection.)

August Swenson was a legendary Swedish immigrant to Texas. He was born in Sweden in 1835 and initially came to Texas with his son, Carl, and his daughter, Mathilda, followed in 1867. He was married to Johanna (Peterson) in Sweden in 1858. When he came to Hutto, he worked as a skilled carpenter and farmer. Swenson was responsible for bringing many other Swedish immigrants to Hutto and helping to begin the Swedish Lutheran Church. Swenson was also the president of the Farmers and Merchants State Bank of Hutto. (Author's collection.)

An early photograph features Swedes eating watermelons. The size of the trees indicates that they were close to a water source and probably having a picnic. Charlotte Spong McCord identified John Spong (fifth from the left) and Axel Spong (sixth from the left). (Courtesy Buddy Holmstrom Collection.)

A. W. Carpenter of Hutto and William M. Woolsey established the first bank in Hutto, the Hutto Bank, in 1892. Carpenter was later coproprietor of the Hutto Bank along with E. P. Wilmot of Austin in 1899. In 1892, A. W. Carpenter was a partner in Carpenter and Woolsey Merchandise in the first brick building constructed on the west side of East Street. (Courtesy Hugh S. Davenport Sr. Collection.)

This is the only known photograph of James D. Tinning's patented cotton planter. This invention received Patent No. 591,613 on October 12, 1897. This was Tinning's only venture into the invention business; however, he was a very successful businessman who partnered with Charles Hanstrom in the waterworks, an ice business, a power plant, and a cotton gin. (Courtesy Jim and Carol Wilson Collection.)

In this 1897 Hutto cotton storage yard photograph, the old Swedish Church is in the background. In 1897, A. W. Carpenter and P. M. Womack were merchants and cotton buyers, and Hal Farley was the cotton weigher. The cotton yard was located on Block 6 of the Railroad Addition now bound by Farley Street, Main Street, Pecan Street, and East Street. (Courtesy Thomas A. Munnerlyn family.)

A Hutto farmer, James D. Tinning Sr., invented a new cotton planter and on May 1897 filed patent No. 591,613 with the U.S. Patent Office in Washington, D.C. His patent was approved on October 12, 1897. Tinning was born in Edinburgh, Scotland, in 1873 and at age 12 immigrated with his family to America. Tinning's invention was said to be the first to allow the operator to raise and lower the sweep and planting mechanism at the same time. (Courtesy Hugh S. Davenport Sr. Collection.)

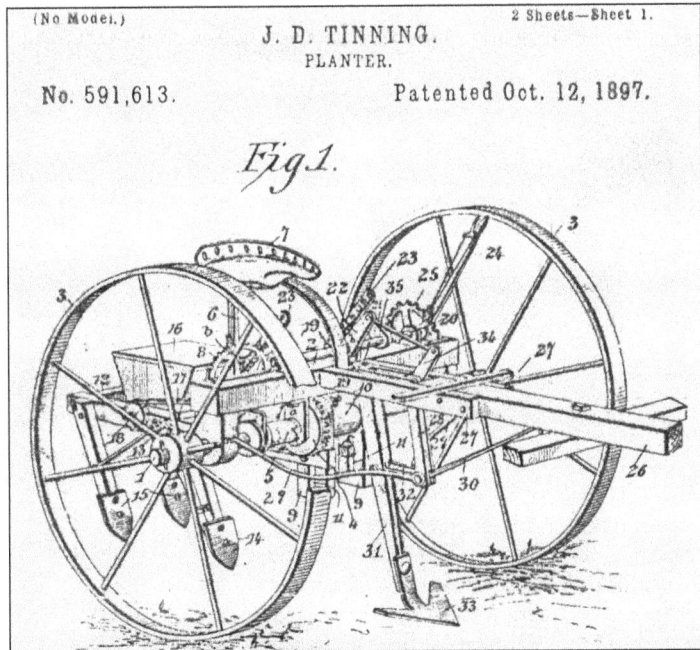

(No Model.)   2 Sheets—Sheet 1.

J. D. TINNING.
PLANTER.

No. 591,613.   Patented Oct. 12, 1897.

Fig.1.

On November 21, 1898, the Hutto Bank received payments in the amount of $120.65 from August Swenson acting on behalf of the Swedish Evangelical Lutheran Church of Hutto as follows: $50 to John Busch (rebate on rent), $45.65 to R. D. Byrom (Williamson County tax collector for taxes), and $25 to Nettie and J. A. Blanton (partial payment on a house located on Lot 9, Block 13). This was toward the purchase of a house as the first parsonage for the above church when Pastor O. H. Sylvan became its first full-time pastor. (Author's collection.)

This receipt from W. D. Holman, a Hutto cotton buyer and later the first mayor of the city of Hutto, to C. J. Wegstrom, a local farmer, is dated September 10, 1895, for 557 pounds of hand-picked cotton at 7½¢ a pound totaling $41.67. (Author's collection.)

Riding horseback on Brushy Creek south of Hutto in the early 1900s are, from left to right, Alex Martin, his brother George Martin, and Werner Kruger in the background. (Courtesy Margaret Crislip Collection.)

This early-1900s photograph of the Gower cotton gin was provided by W. H. Glendenning to the Holman family. Notice the water storage tank. (Courtesy Holman family collection.)

Pastor O. H. and Hilda Serafia Sylvan are here in an early-1900s portrait. Olof H. Sylvan was born in Sweden on February 19, 1854. In the fall of 1883, he immigrated to America, and by early 1890, he was ordained at the Theological Seminary at the Augustana-Synod's College in Rock Island, Illinois. In July 1890, he married Hilda Serafia (Peterson); in October 1899, they came to Hutto, where he was the first full-time pastor of the Hutto Lutheran Church. He was with the Hutto congregation for 14 years and four months until after the death of his wife on May 13, 1913. All sermons and services were in Swedish. (Author's collection.)

In this c. 1900 photograph of influential Hutto citizens on the depot platform are, from left to right, Clara Hanstrom (wife of entrepreneur Charles E. Hanstrom), William H. "Will" Farley Jr. (Hutto Depot agent), John Busch (businessman and owner of the Busch building), Bertha Hanstrom, Mrs. Forest Farley, Celess Dahlberg (daughter of Frank Dahlberg, who had a general merchandise store), John Gilberg, unidentified, Mrs. John Busch, Mrs. Will Farley Jr. (Ava Walling), Nina Arnell, unidentified, Mrs. Womack, Elmer Dahlberg, a son of Frank Dahlberg, and unidentified partial woman at the end. It is known that Ava and W. H. Farley Jr. solicited funds from the community and constructed a new and larger Hutto Depot in 1900 that served the community until it burned in 1945. (Courtesy Hugh S. Davenport Sr. Collection.)

Here is a c. 1900 photograph of people posing at the Hutto Depot. (Courtesy Hugh S. Davenport Sr. Collection.)

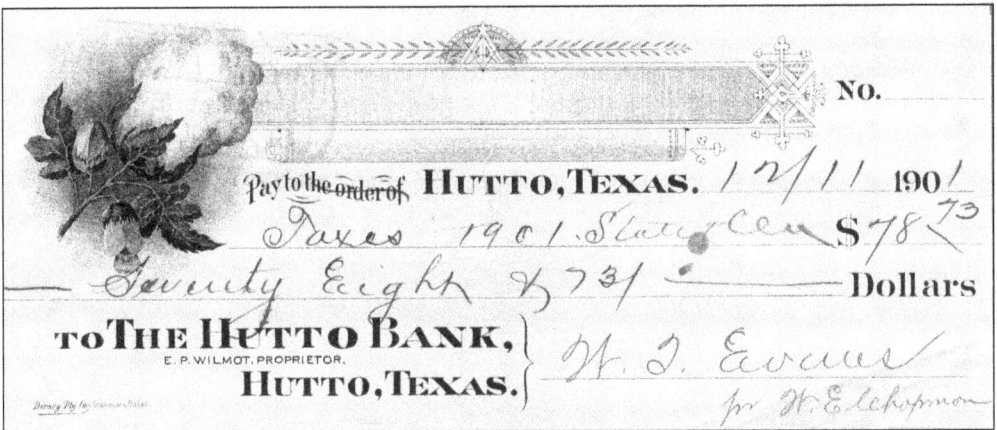

This check from W. T. Evans paid 1901 taxes in the amount of $78.73 on December 12, 1901. The Evans family included some of Hutto's earliest settlers. The Hutto Bank check notes E. P. Wilmot as proprietor of the bank and has a wonderful graphic of a cotton plant in the upper left corner. (Courtesy Hugh S. Davenport Sr. Collection.)

51

Pictured from left to right in this early photograph of the Round Bale Gin are ? Hannah, John Simms, John Barnes, Bill Harkins, George Barnes, and Raymond T. Towns. The man peering over the mule-drawn wooden wagon is unidentified. In the early 1870s, many Swedish immigrants and others came to the black land prairie area and began growing cotton. Many of these immigrants paid for their passage by working several years for those who had paid their passage to America. Those more fortunate bought small farms. (Courtesy Hugh S. Davenport Collection from Lucy Barnes.)

This photograph was taken from on top of a building on East Street looking down Farley Street to the northeast. The house in the top left corner was the Peter Nils Mauritz home. Mauritz was a well-known banker (Farmers and Merchants Bank) in Hutto. Diagonally up from the Mauritz home is the Dr. H. D. Carrington home. The church steeple shown at top left is Hutto Lutheran Church, built in 1892. The Cumberland Presbyterian Church, on the corner of Farley Street and FM (Farm-to-Market Road) 1660, was pastored by the Reverend I. S. Davenport, who was also honored as chaplain of the Senate in the 27th Texas Legislature in 1901. The 1899–1917 two-story wooden Hutto School can be seen at extreme upper right. (Author's collection.)

The Hutto Co-op was one of the strongest visual symbols of Hutto representing the agricultural heritage of the community. Organized and built beginning in 1937, the Hutto Co-op soon became associated with the community identity. In early 2004, the two separate entities owning the approximately 18 acres of property and structures, the Hutto Co-op Gin and the Hutto Co-op Grainery, sold it all to the City of Hutto for $2,050,000. This early-2005 photograph from south of the railroad was taken prior to the city selling off many of these structures for removal during recent years. Not shown are the two cotton gins to the right of these grain structures. (Author's collection.)

A wet day street scene at the Norman Hotel has the wooden sidewalk engulfed in water around 1915. There are three women and three men, all unidentified, on the porch by the "Hotel Office" sign, as indicated by the upward angled lettering in the porch window. Another sign advertises, "For best life insurance see W. M. Norman, Hutto, Texas." Such rain events would bring Hutto to a standstill, as the streets were dirt, or in this case mud, with automobile and horse-and-buggy travel being virtually impossible in the clay-like backland soil. Sometimes burials had to be delayed for many days in extreme wet periods. (Courtesy Hugh S. Davenport Sr. Collection.)

This 1902 photograph of people on East Street illustrates the pioneer and settler spirit that was predominant in Hutto at the time. The first building has two signs, one at the top for "Woolsey & Carpenter," who had a mercantile/dry goods store and also established the first bank in Hutto in 1892. Most of the people wore hats to protect themselves from the Texas sun and heat. Awnings were used on buildings along the entire street to help screen out some of the morning sun. (Courtesy Hugh S. Davenport Sr. Collection.)

Two unidentified ladies in long dresses and white blouses are pictured on the boardwalk in front of the Norman Hotel sign. (Courtesy Hugh S. Davenport Sr. Collection.)

People of Hutto are pictured viewing the damage in a picture taken the day after the disastrous 1902 fire on East Street. The northern half of the east side of the business area on East Street burned down in what was termed "the great fire of Hutto" after a gasoline stove exploded in the Jackson Restaurant. The fire started at about 10:00 on a Saturday evening, and while the hook and ladder company men fought the fire directly on East Street, the women of the community successfully protected the cotton yard, which was being showered with embers. (Courtesy Hutto Chamber of Commerce Collection.)

När ni kommer till Hutto så
förglöm icke att besöka det

Svenska högqvarteret

Det skall glädja oss att få visa eder, hvad vi hafva
att sälja, och ni är alltid välkommen.

Busch, Womack & Hanstrom

This early advertisement in *Texas Posten*, a Swedish newspaper, translates to "When you come to Hutto don't forget to visit the Swedish headquarters. It will be a joy for us to show you what we have to sell, and you are always welcome at Busch, Womack and Hanstrom." From the 1880s through the 1950s, people in Hutto of Swedish heritage were the largest population group. Most Swedish immigrants learned English, but many still held on to their native language. (Courtesy Charles and Clarice Hanstrom Collection.)

Niels Larson was a blacksmith and woodcraftsman of Danish descent who lived in Hutto. In 1900, his business was sold to Soren L. Christianson, who continuously operated it along with his brother, Andrew Christianson, until at least 1958. This 1905 photograph taken in front of the business shows Robert Grek, Tom Short, Nina Barkley (later the second wife of Joseph T. McCutcheon), Nannie Oates, Soren Christianson (next to the post), Peter Martin, W. B. Harrison, George Nehring, and Niels Larson. (Courtesy Hugh S. Davenport Sr. Collection from Alex Martin Sr.)

This photograph from about 1905 shows the Hutto Cornet Band. In the back row are Alex Spong (1879–1965), fourth from left, who was born in Sweden, and John Spong (1884–1945), fifth from left, who was born in Texas. Notice the wonderful hats with HCB on the crest and the drum that is imprinted with Hutto Cornet Band and a star. (Courtesy Rod Johnson Collection.)

This R. B. Spencer and Company bill to Farmers Union Gin Company, dated November 1, 1908, is in the amount of $13.91. One cubic yard of sand cost $2.75, an 8-by-10-inch pane of glass was 10¢, and lumber was very inexpensive, with 21 pieces (1 inch by 8 inches and 12 feet long) costing just $1.68. This lumber company operated for many years in Hutto. (Courtesy Hugh S. Davenport Sr. Collection.)

Flinn and Hutto Dray and Transfer Line billed the Farmers Union Gin Company $728.40 on May 29, 1909, for cement and delivery to build a dam on Cottonwood Creek north of Hutto. A little over 89 cubic yards was sold at $8 per cubic yard. A dray is a strong wagon used to haul goods and materials. A small portion of this 1909 dam still remains today. (Courtesy Hugh S. Davenport Sr. Collection.)

From left to right, Hutto residents Birdie Ray, John Porter (at top), Clyde Ray (below), and Ethel Matthews are posed on and in a wagon. All are wearing hats, and the young ladies are wearing stylish dresses of the day. (Courtesy Hugh S. Davenport Sr. Collection.)

The Norman Hotel was located north of the railroad tracks and close to the Hutto Corner Drug Store on East Street. Pictured are an unidentified hotel guest, Sterling Norman, Hudson Harkins (who stayed at the hotel), Carrie Towns (Sterling's sister), Mrs. William (Mary) Norman, Mary Florence Norman (Mr. and Mrs. Sterling Norman's little girl), Aunt Myrtle (Sterling's sister, married to a Glover and later a Hyslop), Mrs. Sterling Norman, her daughter Viola Norman, W. M. "Boss" Norman, Bill Norman (brother of W. M. Norman), the sister of Mrs. Sterling Norman, and the sister of Mrs. W. M. Norman with her son. (Courtesy Hugh S. Davenport Sr. Collection.)

Edwin Farley, the driver (on the right), and Raymond Towns, the passenger, are posed for this photograph in a convertible automobile with the Norman Hotel in the background. (Courtesy Hugh S. Davenport Sr. Collection.)

At this early Fourth of July get-together on Brushy Creek south of Hutto are, from left to right, (first row) Milfred Wayne Gainer, Milton A. Barnes, Bessie Gene Gainer Barnes, and Barbara Gainer holding R. C. and Janet Gainer's baby; (second row) Billy Jim Edmonds and Joyce Evelyn Gainer Alexander; (third row) Lonnie O. Gainer, Ida Mae Porter Gainer, Alma Irene Gainer Frith Zimmerhanzel, Claudia Elizabeth Hall Morris, Geraldine Barnes Boydston, Grover Milton Gainer (barely showing), Allen Gainer (died at age 16), Edna Wofford Hansen, and Samuel Joseph Gainer; (fourth row) William Floyd Frith, Claude Hall, Melissa Gainer Nash, Sallie Gainer Kennedy, J. B. "Daddy" Gainer, Mrs. Robinson (Bessie Robinson Gainer's mother), R. C. Gainer and wife Janet Gainer, Bessie Robinson Gainer, Hester Winston Gainer, Robert Lee Gainer, Will Nash, and Ruby Bearden Gainer. (Photograph by Lois Gainer; courtesy Hutto Chamber of Commerce Collection.)

Here 15 or more wagons loaded with cotton are being taken in from leased properties for ginning in the background with workers holding saws and hammers on a building project in the foreground. Settlers of the Hutto area were quite industrious and hardworking. (Courtesy Vic and Bertha Stern family collection.)

The Double Gin, also known as the "two at once" gin, was located south of the railroad tracks between FM 1660 South and what is now Jim Cage Sr. Street (formerly Cottonwood Street). The "Big Gin" was owned by Farmers Union, C. N. Stearns, and Hutto Gin Company. Fifteen mostly unidentified working men of Hutto pose in front of the Double Gin. Arthur Olander is standing second from left in his overalls. Pictured above in the loft atop a sign that says "Osgood" are Clarence Ray (left) and Hudson Harkins (right). (Courtesy Isaac "Jock" Norman Collection.)

In this 1910 photograph are Gus Hanson (left) and C. E. Hanstrom, both of Swedish heritage, who were partners of the newly established Hutto Water Works. After a short time, Gus Hanson, a single man, sold his interest to his partner, left Hutto, and was never heard from again. (Courtesy Hugh S. Davenport Sr. Collection.)

Doc Kerley stands at the far right with staff and pupils in this 1911 picture of the Hutto Colored School. In 1901, a group of Christians led by Doc Kerley organized the Ebenezer Baptist Church in Hutto. The church was a primary factor in the education of its youth, and in February 1922, the trustees of Ebenezer Baptist Church planned Kerley Junior High School. The trustees who started the school were Lee Watson, B. Kerley, Wesley Ray, L. Brooks, I. Fresh, and Bart Harrison. (Courtesy Hugh S. Davenport Sr. Collection.)

This c. 1912 photograph shows two unidentified workers at the Hanstrom and Tinning Ice Factory in Hutto. A 25-pound block of ice sold for 10¢. Without the efforts of Charles Evald Hanstrom, Hutto might not have grown as it did. C. E. Hanstrom helped to establish the waterworks, ice factory, electric plant, and electric service for the Hutto community. (Courtesy Charles and Clarice Hanstrom Collection.)

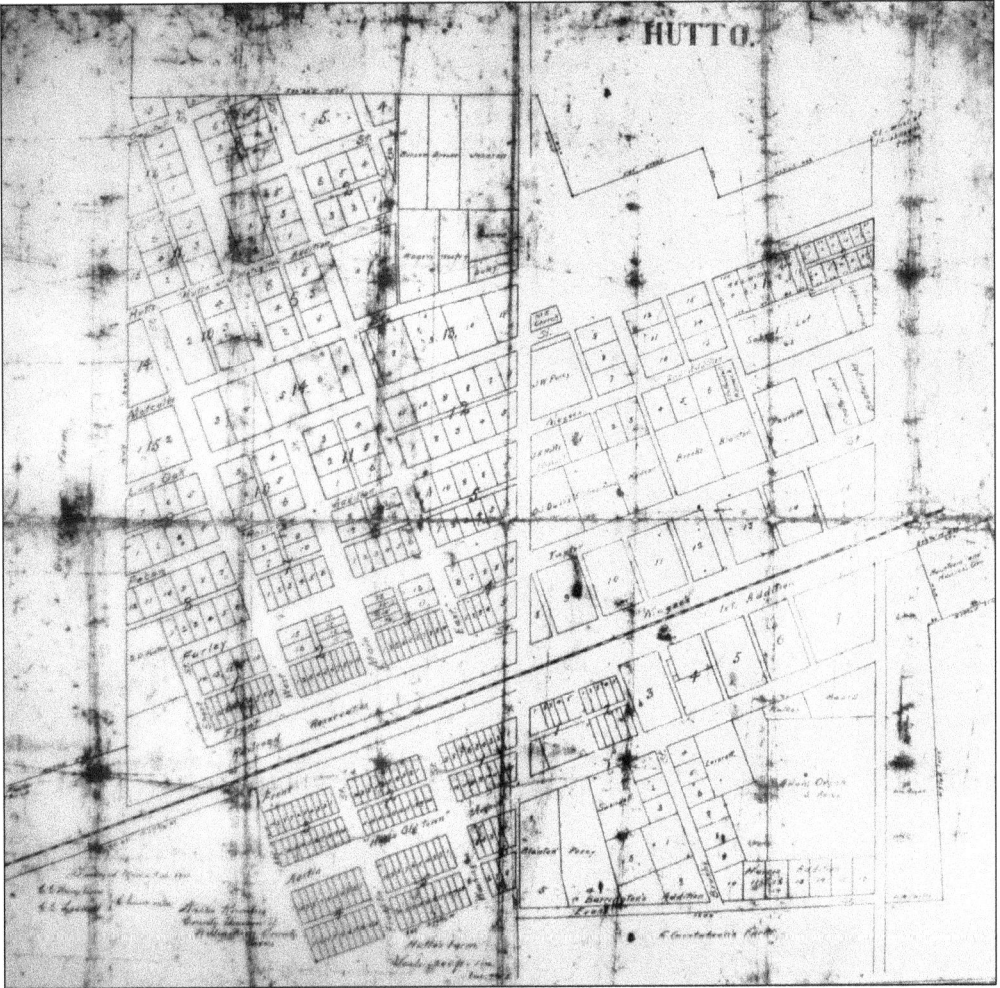

This is a copy of the 1911 incorporation map of the City of Hutto. C. E. Hanstrom and C. E. Lockett, both of Hutto, assisted Walter Rountree, the Williamson County surveyor, on this mapping of Hutto that was certified on March 3, 1911. The map shows items of interest with the southeast 5 acres owned by Adam Organ, correctly spelled Orgain. Adam Orgain, a slave later freed, was the first settler of Hutto in 1854 and eventually purchased this piece of land. Also note that the Hutto Methodist Church was located at the northeast corner of what is now East Live Oak Street and FM 1660 North. (Author's collection.)

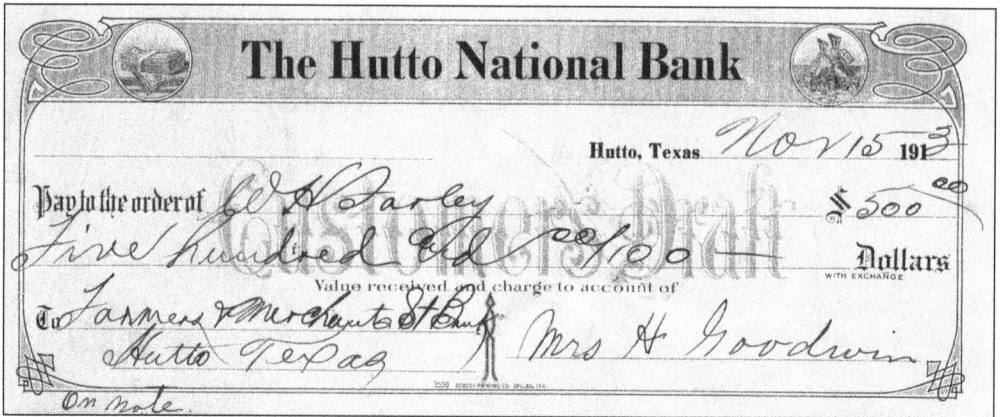

This Hutto National Bank cashier's draft check dated November 15, 1913, in the amount of $500 to W. H. Farley from Mrs. Hugh Goodwin was to be deposited in Farmers and Merchants State Bank, Hutto, as payment "on note." The Goodwin family was purchasing approximately 40 acres north of the railroad and approximately 200 acres south of the railroad all the way down to Brushy Creek from Farley. (Courtesy Hugh S. Davenport Sr. Collection.)

A c. 1915 photograph taken from atop the Hutto Methodist Church looks south down a tree-lined East Street toward the downtown business area. The steeple of the Hutto Presbyterian Church, located on the southwest corner of East and Pecan Streets, is clearly visible. (Courtesy Hugh S. Davenport Sr. Collection from Harvey Olander.)

The Busch Building on East Street was constructed in 1914 by John Busch. In this 1920s photograph, the building was the home to a Humpty Dumpty grocery store with the motto "STOOP-NO-MORE," owned by John Busch, and a hardware store operated by Paul Johnson. When the Humpty Dumpty was relocated to the south portion of the building facing Farley Street, an alligator was kept in the basement and fed meat scraps from the grocery store. These stores closed during the Great Depression. (Courtesy Hutto Chamber of Commerce Collection.)

Rev. I. S. Davenport, pastor of the Cumberland Presbyterian Church beginning in 1898, wears a hat in the dry goods store of a Mr. Riggan on East Street. Note the longleaf pine wood flooring and the pressed-tin ceiling in this approximately 30-foot-wide and 100-foot-long business equipped with well-stocked shelving and a long counter space. (Courtesy Hugh S. Davenport Sr. Collection.)

This is a composite photograph of Swedish homes of Hutto taken from Volume 1 of the original *Svenskarne I Texas 1838–1918* (*Swedes in Texas in Words and Pictures 1838–1918*), which shows some of the fine homes in which Swedish families lived. (Author's collection.)

Three men stand on the wreckage as other people gather following a 1928 train wreck that took place near Hutto the day before Thanksgiving on November 28. A freight train and a passenger train collided; while no one was killed, a number of people were injured. (Courtesy Hutto Chamber of Commerce Collection.)

The Riley Henley café and store are shown on what is now U.S. Highway 79 near FM 1660 North. The box outside advertises Butter Krust Bread, made by Austin Baking Company. To the east in the right portion of the picture was the Spencer Lumber Company. The Hutto café was operated by Riley Henley with the help of her brother Will Henley. (Courtesy Charles and Clarice Hanstrom Collection.)

Pictured from left to right in this early Hutto Meat Market photograph are Joe Bernal (slaughterer), R. B. "Bert" Payne Sr. (owner and butcher), Spencer Goodwin, Sam Downing, and Will Goodwin. R. B. Payne Sr. was also engaged in farming and as a cotton buyer during his career. (Courtesy Buddy Holmstrom Collection.)

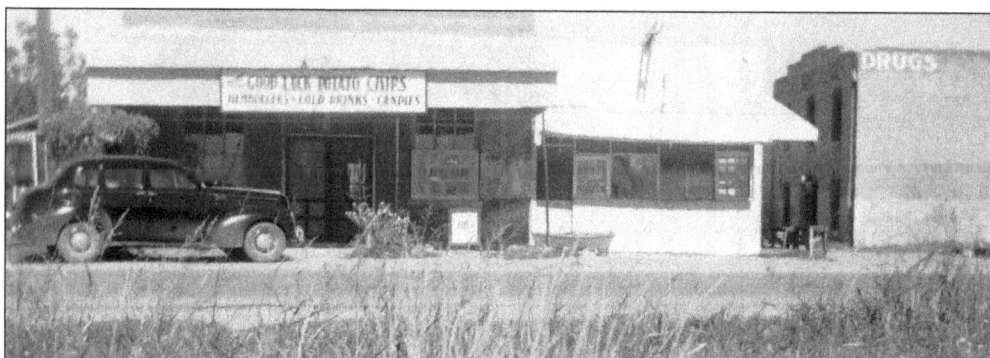

The Good Luck Potato Chips building, owned and operated by Riley Henley, is pictured with her Studebaker located to the left by today's U.S. Highway 79. From this site, she also operated a café selling hamburgers, cold drinks, and candies. (This building had also served as a funeral parlor; in recent times, it was the home of Snuffy's Bar and Grill.) At one time, Riley Henley made fresh potato chip deliveries in her Studebaker to Hutto, Taylor, Granger, and Thrall and sold paper bags of chips for 5¢ a bag. The white structure was an ice and snow cone shop operated by her brother Will Henley and located in what is now known as Snuffy's Alley. The building on the right was the back of Hutto Drug Store on the southwest corner of East Street and U.S. Highway 79. (Courtesy Charles and Clarice Hanstrom.)

This 1928 photograph is of the 17 boys on the football team coached by D. J. Wilkins. Second from left in the first row is Ralph Applin. In the second row are (second from left) G. W. "Cub" Nelson and (far right) Levi Adams. In the third row are (third from left) Arnold "Pete" Johnson, (fifth from left) Harvey Payne, and (sixth from left) Gunnar Johnson. In 1928, Hutto School went only to the 11th grade for graduation. (Courtesy Charlie and Clarice Hanstrom Collection.)

Sixteen men of Hutto, all wearing hats, are pictured in this early photograph. In the first row at far left is Sammie Downing, and sixth from left is Hudson Harkins, the only man with no coat. In the top row, third from the left, is Charles Hanstrom Sr. as a young man. (Courtesy Hutto Chamber of Commerce Collection.)

The Midget Café in Hutto was located at the corner of East Street and U.S. Highway 79. The man behind the counter is proprietor Jim Patterson. The Midget Café advertised in the 1930 *Hutto Herald* newspaper: "Where Service is a Pleasure, Our Dinner is Our Specialty, Our Coffee is Our Pride." (Courtesy Hugh S. Davenport Sr. Collection.)

This is the Friskey Lynch and Otis Whitely gas station, located on FM 1660 North in Hutto. (Courtesy Hugh S. Davenport Sr. Collection.)

The Johnson grocery store at 206 Farley Street is photographed with, from left to right, Paul Johnson, unidentified, Charlie "Pete" Johnson (mayor of Hutto in the 1930s) with what appears to be a Coca-Cola in his hand, and two unidentified subjects. (Courtesy Hugh S. Davenport Sr. Collection.)

This is an early interior photograph of Hutto Farmers and Merchants State Bank on the northwest corner of East and Farley Streets. August Swenson was the founder and first president of the bank. From left to right are Walter Swenson, Eric Brown, and W. D. Holman in the bow tie holding his pipe. Holman was the first mayor of Hutto. Note the pressed-tin ceiling, the teller cages, and the ceramic tile flooring that was original to the bank. Later this building also served for many years as the Hutto Post Office. (Courtesy Hugh S. Davenport Sr. Collection.)

Here is the interior of Miller Brothers Store in Hutto during the 1920s; it was operated by Sid Miller, another mayor of Hutto. Miller stands toward the back of his well-stocked store with two unidentified ladies. The store was a men and women's store and grocery store combination located at 115 East Street. The building is currently owned by another past mayor, Edmund Schmidt, who along with his wife, Julia, operated another grocery store at 117 East Street for 40 years. (Courtesy Hugh S. Davenport Sr. Collection.)

The IGA grocery store was owned and operated by Roy Anderson. The Independent Grocers Alliance was started in May 1926 in the United States and is now worldwide. Pictured from left to right are Amelia Hennech, Roy Anderson (mayor of Hutto from 1948 to 1954), and Bennie Downing in the background. (Courtesy Hutto Chamber of Commerce Collection.)

Snuffy's was a longtime Hutto institution located in an old historic building at 204 U.S. Highway 79. For many years, Snuffy's Bar and Grill had live music every Saturday and an interesting local and biker clientele. The building interior was remodeled and in late 2007 became Fat Thompson's Sports Bar and Grill. Back in the late 1890s and early 1900s, it was a funeral home with Mrs. L. E. Bostic as undertaker and with a horse-drawn hearse stored inside. (Author's collection.)

Clarence Ray (the previous postmaster, in background) and Oscar Humphrey (postmaster, in front) are at the Hutto Post Office, then located at 202 Earley Street. The Hutto Post Office was established June 27, 1877. First-class postage was 3¢ at the time this photograph was taken. The postmasters of Hutto are James E. Hutto (1877–1879), John A. Blanton (1879–1883), Thomas M. Metcalfe (1883–1890), William H. McCormick (1890–1891), Victor M. McCormick (1891–1893), Thomas H. Flinn (1893–1897), Joseph P. Ross (1897–1909), J. R. Davis (1909–1911), Lillie Wilson (1911–1916), Willis D. Holman (1916–1924), John Clarence Ray (1924–1933), Ward O. Miller (1933–1934), Walter L. Bergstrom (1934–1938), Oscar Humphrey (1938–1952), Carl Stern (1952–1953), Hugh S. Davenport (1953–1975), W. C. Welch (1975–1985), Mary Srnensky (1985–2006), and Cindy West (2007–present). (Courtesy Hugh S. Davenport Sr. Collection.)

Three

HUTTO'S RICH HISTORY

This is an early livestock photograph with six horses. People of Scottish heritage are, from left to right, Jim Tinning, a small unidentified child, "Granny" Bess Martin, and William Martin. (Courtesy Margaret Crislip Collection.)

This two-story wooden school was the third school built in Hutto and served education needs from 1899 until 1917, according to Harvey Olander. It only went through the 10th grade. The first small school was destroyed by a tornado that wiped out many of the south-side structures on June 19, 1886. This tornado prompted a major decision to rebuild the town on the north side of the railroad tracks. (Courtesy Hugh S. Davenport Sr. Collection.)

This early photograph is titled "Street Scene, Hutto, Texas" and was taken on what is now Pecan Street and FM 1660 North looking north. To the left front is the Mauritz home, now the bed-and-breakfast Das Winkler Haus; to the right is the Dr. H. D. Carrington house with the American Methodist Church of Hutto and a large barn in the background. (Courtesy Hugh S. Davenport Sr. Collection.)

This early photograph, titled "South M. E. Church Hutto, Tex.," is of the American Methodist Church of Hutto in the left foreground and the Hutto Evangelical Lutheran Church, built in 1902, in the right background (Courtesy Hugh S. Davenport Sr. Collection.)

The Hutto Methodist Church started as the Methodist Episcopal Church or "Swedish Methodists" in the late 1800s. A small group of Swedish immigrant families held services entirely in Swedish in the church they built in 1882. By 1910, the new church pictured above was completed at its East Street location. In 1938, the pastor and elders of the Swedish Methodist Church invited the Methodist Episcopal Church to merge with them. The two churches joined as the Hutto Methodist Church and held their first service on the first Sunday of November 1938. Through additional mergers, the church eventually became Discovery United Methodist Church. (Courtesy Hugh S. Davenport Sr. Collection.)

The 1916 Hutto baseball team posted a perfect season record of 26-0. In this photograph are, from left to right, (first row) Bernie Hutto, Ike Brown, Dago Nelson, and William Rudolph Bowden; (second row) Lynn Nichols, Theodore Eklund, Buddy Robinson, Roy Holman (manager/coach), Emsy Saul, Hatton Nelson, and Henry Eklund. Roy Holman is wearing a cowboy hat and has a watch chain/fob attached to his belt. Players Ike Brown and Dago Nelson are holding cigarettes in their hands, and William Rudolph Bowden has a box of "Yum Yums." (Courtesy Buddy Holmstrom Collection.)

This World War I photograph of Jim Glendenning of Hutto in his wool army uniform was taken by J. Santcross, the Camp Dix official photographer, as embossed on the picture and coded R2 9/11. The collar buttons and cap indicated that Jim was in the 134th Infantry. (Courtesy Margaret Crislip Collection.)

1917 TO 1937

This three-story redbrick school building served from 1917 until 1937 and, according to both Harvey Olander and Betty Sue Blackman Holmstrom in her book, *Hutto and Hippos*, was the fourth Hutto school. Holmstrom wrote, "The first floor contained four classrooms and the second floor had four classrooms, the office and the library. On the third floor was the auditorium and two dressing rooms." (Courtesy Hugh S. Davenport Sr. Collection.)

This is a studio photograph of George Martin of Hutto in his woolen World War I uniform with leather leggings. Shortly after returning to Hutto following the war, George Martin was killed in a cotton ginning accident in Hutto. (Courtesy Margaret Crislip Collection.)

The First Baptist Church of Hutto was established in 1882 by Rev. Abram Weaver and Joseph Granda with 13 members. The church originally met in the school and in 1883 built three churches (two of which were destroyed by storms), all located south of the railroad tracks. In 1922, the Hutto Baptist Church pictured was built north of the railroad tracks at Main and Farley Streets. Hutto Baptist Church relocated to 6655 U.S. Highway 79. (Author's collection.)

This is a 1982 picture of the Little Ebenezer Baptist Church at 215 South Brushy Street. The church was founded in 1901 when a group of Christians led by Doc Kerley organized the Ebenezer Baptist Church in Hutto. For many years, Ebenezer Baptist Church was led by Rev. C. J. McClain until his death in 1968. In 1969, Ebenezer Baptist Church merged with Little Bethel Baptist Church, led by Rev. Edward Mercer, pastor. He was followed by Rev. Cecil H. Young, and the newly merged congregation was then named Little Ebenezer Baptist Church. (Courtesy Hugh S. Davenport Sr. Collection.)

Discovery United Methodist Church of Hutto began as the Methodist Episcopal Church or "Swedish Methodists" in the late 1800s. In 2004, the Hanson family donated 10 acres of land on what is now Ed Schmidt Boulevard, and Discovery United Methodist Church began planning to move and restore the 1910 sanctuary at their new location. On March 16, 2008, the Discovery United Methodist Church held its first service in their restored sanctuary. (Author's collection.)

New Hope Christian Church celebrates at the pavilion in Fritz Park with a hot air balloon on Sunday, March 29, 2009. (Author's collection.)

Two unidentified men and a 1920s car are shown in this rare heavy snowfall photograph taken in December 1929 at the Blackman Garage. It was advertised that Magnolia gas, Quaker State oil, and Goodyear tires were sold at the garage/filling station. (Courtesy Hugh S. Davenport Sr. Collection.)

Most of the 1923 graduating class of Hutto High School is pictured here. From left to right are (squatting) Supt. W. E. Gattis; (seated) Harry Johnson, Frank Petwey Highsmith, Isahm Roscoe Lister, Walter Alfred "Joe" Nelson, and Owen Renshaw Flinn; (kneeling) Katherine Tinning, Pauline Gertrude Peterson, Birdie Lee Barnes, Myrtle Peterson, Dora Estella Johnson, and Alice Anderson; (standing) Irene Odes Johnson, Alice Ruth "Annie" Anderson, Eva Marie Nelson (class of 1922), Etoyle Bartlett Stephens (class of 1922), Bernyce Irene Blackman, Louetta Cearley, Bessie Eugenia Gainer, Francis Miller, Hazel Azile Shugart, ? Leggett, and Minnie Downing. The class of 1922 had only two graduates. (Courtesy Hugh S. Davenport Sr. Collection.)

Supt. Walter "W. E." Gattis poses with his Chevrolet automobile in front of the Hutto School. Below the license plate is another plate that has "Hutto, Texas" on it. Gattis served as school superintendent from 1921 to 1927. This three-story redbrick school was constructed in 1917 and was the primary educational facility for the Hutto community until 1937. (Courtesy Hugh S. Davenport Sr. Collection.)

Darrell "Sam" Blackman is seen here as a small child playing next to Pecan Street in his pedal car. Sam Blackman was later a coach at Hutto and served during World War II. In the background to the left is the old Porter Walker and later Alfred and LaVerne Reinhardt home at 202 East Pecan Street, now owned by Robert and Sarah Tober. (Courtesy Hugh S. Davenport Sr. Collection.)

Bertha Spong Swanson, born in 1911, is on a visit to Texas in 1928 from Kansas City. She was photographed in the back by the automobile while in Hutto cotton fields with unidentified field hands and relatives. (Courtesy Rod Johnson Collection from Bertha Spong Swanson.)

The Jake's Hill Bridge is now gone, replaced by a newer structure; however, its memories live on through images and stories of Jake's Hill. This old crossing at County Road 137 (also known as Jake's Hill Road) and Brushy Creek still has a reputation for being haunted. Local lore has it that Jake killed his wife and two children and then hanged himself from the bridge. Supposedly, if someone parked a car in neutral, Jake would push the car across the flat bridge. (Courtesy Ron Whitfield Collection.)

A late-morning photograph shows Hutto men at the Blackman Garage in the early 1930s. Along with gasoline sales, Goodyear tires and Chevrolet sales and service were also available. From left to right are (first row) Alex Blackman, Alex Martin, "Little" Ed Johnson, Jack Blackman, Ely Blackman, and John Henneck; (second row) Jack Martin, Forrest Blackman, Carl Hammer, Dutch Blackman, John Stevens, Harvey Payne, Aubrey Blackman, Leslie Blackman, and Dave Barnes. The man in the background is unidentified. (Courtesy Margaret Crislip Collection.)

Mae and Sid Miller are at their home on West Live Oak Street. Sid Miller was a mayor of Hutto and also jointly operated Miller Brothers, a men's store and grocery store located in the second building to the south on the west side of East Street at Farley Street. (Courtesy Hugh S. Davenport Sr. Collection.)

This is a 1930s photograph of Carl Johan Wegstrom with his chickens on his property that went from Live Oak Street through to Metcalfe Street. The Wegstrom family had their home, an outhouse, a garage, a tool shed, a cistern, a garden, and a barn for their cows and goats. (Author's collection.)

This is an early-1931 family portrait of the J. J. Swindoll family at their farm south of Hutto. Ann (mother) and Jesse J. Swindoll (father) pose with their children, from left to right, Margaret, Beth, and Warren. The Swindoll family has long been a part of the fabric and history of Hutto. (Courtesy Margaret Crislip Collection.)

Jim Higgans Holman (class of 1931) was the mayor of Hutto from April 1954 until April 1958 and helped to bring sewer to the city of Hutto in 1956, when the city also purchased the waterworks. Jim Holman was involved in a farming partnership and was the son of Hutto's first mayor, Willis D. Holman. One story has it that while in school he came up with "Hippos" as the name of the school mascot. (Courtesy Holman family collection.)

Carl Stern lassoes a cow by the barn on the family farm. The Stern family was from Germany, and Stern means "star" in German. Carl Stern was selected as the first Chamber Citizen of the Year in 1987 at the first Hutto Chamber of Commerce banquet. (Courtesy Carl and Lois Stern Collection.)

This is an early-1930s photograph of a young Charlie "Bus" Hanstrom dressed in matching overalls and ball cap by his family's automobile (Texas 264-805) at the Hanstrom and Tinning Gin. The cotton gin was originally a coal-powered processing plant. Beginning in 1930, at 10 years of age, the young Charlie worked at the cotton gin marking wagons with numbers as they came in to keep them in order and was paid $1 a day for his work. (Courtesy Charles and Clarice Hanstrom Collection.)

Construction for the Hutto School is seen in this Depression-era 1937 photograph. The contractors were, from left to right, J. R. Blackmon and Roland Blackmon along with their workers. (Courtesy Hugh S. Davenport Sr. Collection.)

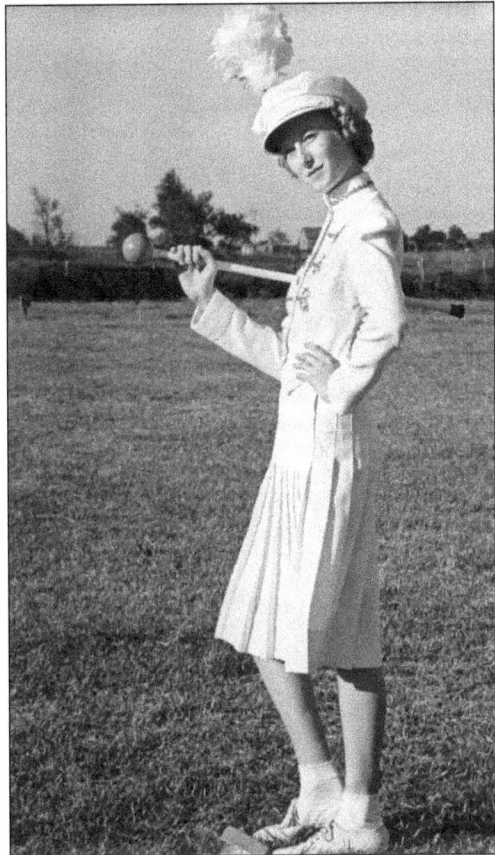

Margaret Swindoll was drum major for Hutto High School from 1938 to 1940. The football field at that time was Spencer Goodwin's pasture. Margaret was later a fashion model in Washington, D.C., New York, and Dallas. On July 17, 1947, Margaret married Sgt. Maj. James Crislip, who served in the U.S. Army for 33 years. (Courtesy Margaret Crislip Collection.)

No. 27 Isaac "Jock" Norman (class of 1942), Hutto team cocaptain and quarterback; No. 24 Brent Bergstrom (class of 1942), Hutto team cocaptain and lineman/kicker; and their football coach, C. E. "Puggy" Smith, who was originally from Georgetown, are seen here in 1941. (Courtesy Buddy Holmstrom Collection.)

Posing in May 1943 are Thomas "T. G." Muir, the superintendent of Hutto School, and Mrs. J. C. (Bertha) Ray, the principal of Hutto School. Thomas Muir served from 1941 until 1944. Ray assisted in the education of the children of Hutto from the 1920s until 1934 as a teacher and from 1934 until 1946 as the principal. (Courtesy Hugh S. Davenport Sr. Collection.)

The Hutto Hippos 1944 basketball team included (first row) second from left Doyle Lindgren (class of 1945) and second from right Carroll Holmstrom (class of 1947); (second row) fourth from left Kermit Johnson and fifth from left Elgene "Buddy" Holmstrom (class of 1944). (Courtesy Rod Johnson Collection.)

The 1944 Hutto football backfield players were No. 33 quarterback Victor H. "Vic" Stern (class of 1945), No. 41 fullback Nelson C. Johnson (class of 1945), No. 99 halfback James T. "Jimmy" Eulenfield (class of 1945), and No. 44 halfback Doyle Lindgren (class of 1945). Vic Stern explained that wartime shortages meant that sometimes a player had to be adaptable, and the 16-man football squad once rode for 30 miles in a cotton trailer to play the Briggs v. Hutto game—in a cow pasture. (Courtesy Vic and Bertha Stern family collection.)

This 1945 photograph was taken looking to the southeast of a burned Hutto Depot. This was the second depot for Hutto and was constructed in 1900. (Courtesy Hugh S. Davenport Sr. Collection.)

Here is a World War II photograph of Hutto men Charlie Hanstrom (left) and Harry Hanson posing by an Alaskan "Flying Tiger" aircraft assigned to the group commanded by Maj. John Chennault, son of General Chennault, commander of the "Flying Tigers" in China. This photograph of Hanstrom and Hanson was taken while they were stationed on the Aleutian Islands off the coast of Alaska. Lifelong friends, both entered the service following Pearl Harbor in January 1942 as mechanics in the U.S. Army Air Corps. (Courtesy Charles and Clarice Hanstrom Collection.)

Sgt. Howard "Jazz" Norman was a radio operator/gunner in the Army Air Corps during World War II. Norman (class of 1940) was born on February 27, 1922, and was reported MIA (missing in action) on July 2, 1943, while part of a B-24 crew returning from a mission in the Pacific theater in Burma. Neither the plane nor crew was ever found, and in 1946, Howard Norman was declared legally dead. (Courtesy Isaac "Jock" Norman Collection.)

Cpl. Edmund Schmidt served his country from December 1942 until October 1945 as a U.S. Army medic during World War II. He assisted with several evacuations of American prisoners of the Japanese. He said that some of the men were little more than "skeletons with skin over them." (Courtesy Schmidt family collection.)

Harvey Oswald Payne (Hutto High class of 1929) served as a military public relations officer; he is here with his wife, Mary (Brown) Payne. After World War II, Harvey served as a press secretary for Congressman Lyndon Baines Johnson. (Courtesy Buddy Holmstrom Collection.)

Vic Stern proudly shows his U.S. Air Force uniform. Victor Henry Stern was born on September 27, 1927, and graduated in a class of 14 from Hutto High School on May 25, 1945. Vic joined the Army Air Corps, was honorably discharged, and came home to Hutto, where he lived his entire life except for his Korean War–era service to his country. Vic has been highly involved in the community through the Hutto Lions Club, Hutto Lutheran Church, the Hutto Volunteer Fire Department, the Hutto City Council, and the Hutto Independent School District Board. (Courtesy Vic and Bertha Stern family collection.)

The 1947 Hutto fast-pitch baseball team was photographed after taking first place and winning the District 9 championship. Pictured from left to right are (seated) Jack Blackman, Pap Moore, Jim Holman, Buddy Holmstrom, Carroll Holmstrom, Charles Hanstrom, Dilbert Decker, Dago Nelson, and batboy/mascot David Holmstrom; (standing) Ed Lawhon, Carl Stern, Isam "Ike" Coward, Carl Everett Lidell, Vic Stern, and Sam Blackman. (Courtesy Charles and Clarice Hanstrom Collection.)

Facing the northeast in the fall of 1947, cotton wagons and trailers wait for processing with several vehicles at the Hutto Co-op Cotton Gin No. 1, the large structure in the back. The small building in the left foreground was a small café/snack bar originally operated by Mrs. Walter Hyslop and later others. (Courtesy Hugh S. Davenport Sr. Collection.)

The upper part of the Hutto Co-op Cotton Gin No. 1 is seen in this fall 1947 photograph as the cotton trailers and wagons await ginning of their contents. The road south of the gin is now U.S. Highway 79, and train cars can be seen on the railroad tracks. (Courtesy Hugh S. Davenport Sr. Collection.)

In this August 1949 photograph, the Hutto Co-op cotton gin has been badly burned by fire started by a lightning strike. Because this was a prime period for cotton ginning, the Hutto Co-op rebuilt and was able to resume ginning that same year. (Courtesy Carl and Lois Stern Collection.)

This is an August 1949 photograph taken from the southeast of the Stern homestead on the family farm located one-half mile west of the 1911 incorporated city of Hutto. This beautiful 1907 Victorian farmhouse was moved into the west side old town area of Hutto in 2001 by Dennis and Donna (Stern) Slocum as their home. For many years, it was the home of Donna's grandparents, Lydia and Charles Stern. (Courtesy Carl and Lois Stern Collection.)

This 1949 photograph is of two Swedish brothers: David "Red" Oman (class of 1959, Hutto High School) holding the bucket and his younger sibling, Richard Arlen Oman (class of 1961, Hutto High School), at ages 10 and 8 on the family farm west of Hutto. (Courtesy David "Red" Oman Collection.)

A Homecoming dance was held in the gymnasium at Hutto High School in November 1950. Chaperones at the dance were Billie and Hugh Davenport and Ruby and Bennie Downing. (Courtesy Hugh S. Davenport Sr. Collection.)

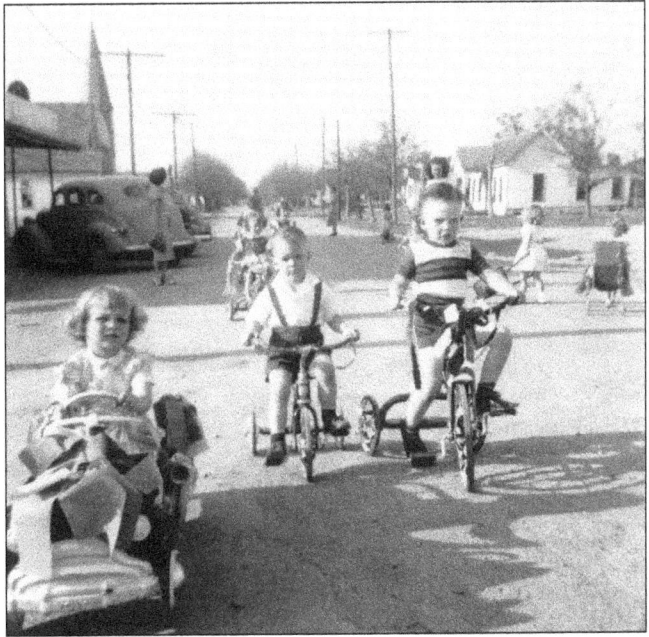

Hutto children take over East Street at the intersection of Farley Street in March 1951 with their decorated mechanical car, tricycles, stroller, and play wheelbarrow. According to Skip Davenport, "The boy on the right is Jimmy Ray Johnson who lived in the house now occupied by the Florence Winkler. The girl in front is Aleda (Hanstrom) Crislip. I'm the guy in the middle riding a tricycle. The church is the old Presbyterian Church which disbanded when I was about five or six years old and torn down a few years later . . . probably late 50s." (Courtesy Hugh S. Davenport Sr. Collection.)

Families enjoy a community Easter hunt put on by the Hutto Volunteer Fire Department in April 1984. The Hutto Volunteer Fire Department dedicated the Hutto Fire Hall in the background on October 22, 1983. (Author's collection.)

Pictured here are members of the Hutto Lions Club at the Charter Night Banquet on March 22, 1954. From left to right are (first row) Emory Stromberg, Noel Grisham, E. S. Johnson, Jim H. Holman, Pete Gainer, M. A. Barnes, and Emery "Dutch" Blackman; (second row) Carl Stromberg, Hugh S. Davenport, Roy L. Anderson, Elgene "Buddy" Holmstrom, Bill Johnson, Kermit A. Johnson, and Carroll Holmstrom; (third row) Anton "Tony" Franzen, Isham A. Coward, Charles E. "Charlie" Hanstrom, Warren Percy, Edmund S. "Ed" Schmidt, H. L. "Harvey" Barrow, Clyde Taylor, and Henry Hooper Jr. Other charter members not shown are Walter Albert, Merle F. Carlson, John Harper, Guy Inman, V. C. Johnson, V. L. Smith, Lambert Johnson, Joe Hensley, Roy E. Malone, Clyde Majors, and H. K. Shackelford. (Courtesy Buddy Holmstrom Collection.)

This January 1957 photograph of the Cub Scouts of Hutto and their sponsors includes, from left to right, Scouts Ricky Ward, Larry Townsend, Eric Johnson, Tony Franzen, Emory Leshber, John Noren, Bubba Franzen, Skip Davenport, Jimmy Campbell, Jimmie Ray Johnson, Chan Priest, and Marvin Gola; adults Mrs. Anton (Dorothy) Franzen (den mother), Virgil Carlson (Cubmaster), and Mrs. Hugh (Billie) Davenport Sr. (den mother). (Courtesy Hugh S. Davenport Sr. Collection.)

Waiting grain trucks and trailers are lined up all along Farley Street all the way back to FM 1660 North in this July 1955 photograph. (Courtesy Hugh S. Davenport Sr. Collection.)

The Hutto All-Star Team played in the 1958 World Softball Championship Tournament sponsored by the International Softball League, Inc., held in Long Beach, California. Those pictured here not from Hutto are from the central Texas area. From left to right are (first row) Emery "Dutch" Blackman (manager/coach, Hutto), T. W. Holmstrom (Hutto), Clayton Dugger, Ronnie Wallace (batboy), George "Bubba" Barnes (Hutto), and Edwin Lawhon (Hutto); (second row) Dickey Gonzales, Emory Teichelman (Hutto), Gilbert Wallace, Buddy Holmstrom (Hutto), Doyle Lindgren (Hutto), Carroll Holmstrom (Hutto), Don Cavness (later a state representative from Austin), Vernon Kunshick, and Daniel "Rat" Sorenson (Hutto). (Courtesy Buddy Holmstrom Collection.)

Quarterback Jeremy Kerley takes the ball as Hutto defeats Taylor in the fall of 2006 at Hippo Stadium. (Author's collection.)

The Carl and Lois Stern family poses in the early 1960s. Carl was a technical engineer for KTBC in Austin, served two years on the Hutto City Council, and was mayor for another eight years. He also was the City of Hutto chief financial officer for 30 years. Lois (Zehner) Stern managed her family and a career in hospital housekeeping. Children are, from left to right, Robert "Bob" Charles Stern (now a renowned pathologist), "John" Mark Stern (an attorney/certified public accountant with the State of Texas Office of the Attorney General), Daniel "Dan" Ray Stern (an attorney with a prestigious law firm), and Mary Ann (Stern) Whitfield (a respected special education teacher). (Courtesy Carl and Lois Stern Collection.)

In August 1962 at the Hutto Co-op cotton gin are, from left to right, Marshall Ford and Pete Hanusch both with their heads down, Woodrow Huggland, and Jim Gainer working on a newly banded bale of cotton. (Courtesy Hutto Chamber of Commerce Collection.)

This late-1960s aerial photograph of the Hutto Grain Co-op and the Hutto Co-op Gin was taken from a small aircraft to the south of the MoPac railroad tracks and U.S. Highway 79. (Courtesy Hutto Chamber of Commerce Collection.)

David "Red" Oman (class of 1959) shows his second-place heavyweight-division champion steer from the Williamson County Livestock Show held in Taylor in 1959. His brother, Richard, had the grand champion heavyweight steer that same year. (Courtesy David "Red" Oman Collection.)

A sign of changing times, the last of the livestock in the Hutto City Limits is loaded up from Curtis Peterson's barn area. Ron Whitfield, a next-door neighbor of Curtis Peterson, assisted in loading Curtis Peterson's two bulls and three cows into a cattle trailer on April 15, 2009, from the pasture and barn located near Hutto and Main Streets. (Author's collection.)

In a 1973 photograph of daughters and their mother, from left to right are Erlinda, Lupe, Elvira, Rose, Delores, Anita, Teresa, and their mother, Mary Ann Aguilar, chopping cotton on a Hutto farm off of County Road 110. (Courtesy Mario and Mary Ann Aguilar Collection.)

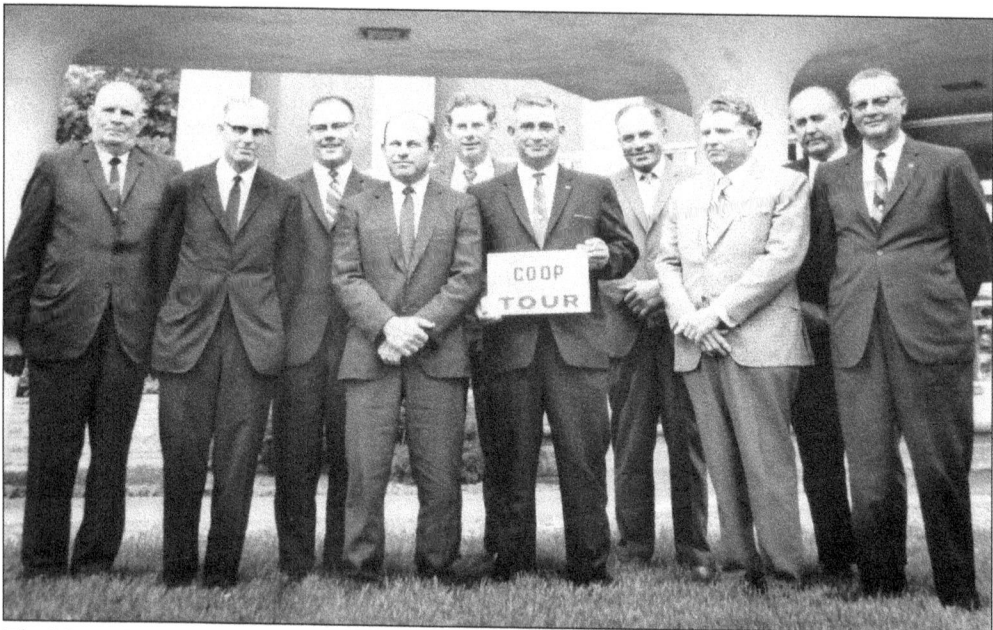

The Hutto Co-op Board tour in the 1970s included, from left to right, Alvin Anderson, Marshall Ford, Kenneth Johnson, Vic Stern, the Co-op tour representative (not from Hutto), Arnold Leschber, Harry Hanson, Jerry Roznovak, Isedor Wallin, and Fred Klaus. (Courtesy Hutto Chamber of Commerce Collection.)

Vic Stern is on his family farm harvesting fields of cotton with his tractor harvester rig and trailer. Vic Stern has been involved in Hutto agriculture his entire life. On January 10, 1951, Vic married Bertha Anderson, and they had six children: Vickie (1952), Donna (1953), Bill (1956), Elaine (1957), Beth (1964), and Lisa (1967). (Courtesy Vic and Bertha Stern family collection.)

The Hutto Lumber Company (once the R. B. Spencer and Company lumber and hardware store) is seen in this early-1980s photograph and was owned and operated by W. H. Bearden, then sold to Vic Stern and finally to Cockrum Cabinets and Countertops. The 16,000-square-foot wooden frame and metal-clad building burned to the ground on August 19, 1987. (Courtesy Hugh S. Davenport Sr. Collection.)

The 1981 Santa Lucia celebration, a winter-light festival that takes place during the darkest time of the year, is held at Hutto Lutheran Church. This event is traditionally held every year in Sweden on December 13. From left to right are Barbara Shepard, Paula Almquist, Michelle Stromberg (Santa Lucia wearing a crown of lights), Rhonda Exley, and Sandy Sakewitz with Donna Fowler as narrator. (Author's collection.)

On March 1, 1982, the old Etol Ecklund house, a two-story Victorian home originally built by this Swedish family in the early 1900s on Jim Cage Sr. Avenue near Front Street, burned to the ground. Ron Whitfield, pictured above, was one of the volunteer firefighters responding to the blaze. (Author's collection.)

Pictured here is an early pre–Hutto Chamber of Commerce ribbon cutting in February 1986 for Juanita's Business Services and the *Hutto Heritage*, a small weekly community information publication. From left to right are Dr. Ernie Lawrence, Pastor Charles Mantey, Pat Stromberg, Mike Fowler, Julia Schmidt, Mayor Edmund Schmidt, Mary Schneider, Mert Hackett, Sharon Fritz, Juanita Rosplock, Dona and Tristan Almquist, Jerry Rosplock, Julian Almquist, unidentified, Mary Mager, Eva Melton, and Dale Alley. (Author's collection.)

The City of Hutto government was located at 103 East Street for many years. Before this location, it was common for the city secretary to keep the city records in his or her home. At the time of this picture, the Hutto Volunteer Fire Department was housed in the back of the building, the City of Hutto was in the front, and the Hutto Lions Club convened upstairs. (Author's collection.)

Intense flames and black smoke fill the sky as the Cockrum Cabinets and Countertops business burns in August 1987. (Courtesy Hugh S. Davenport Sr. Collection.)

In 1987, these trailers, full of cotton, are ready for processing and baling prior to a module system of processing the cotton. Vic Stern was the board president of the Hutto Co-op Gin from the mid-1960s until 1978 and then general manager of the Hutto Gin Co-op from 1978 to 1989. (Courtesy Vic and Bertha Stern family collection.)

Some of the Hutto Players, a local theatrical group, are seen here. They met in the East Street Dining and Social Club, then at 111 East Street. From left to right are Mary Ellen Milburn, Nancy Dupertius, Dennis Dobias, Mary Schneider, and Donna Fowler beginning rehearsals for the female version of *The Odd Couple*. (Author's collection.)

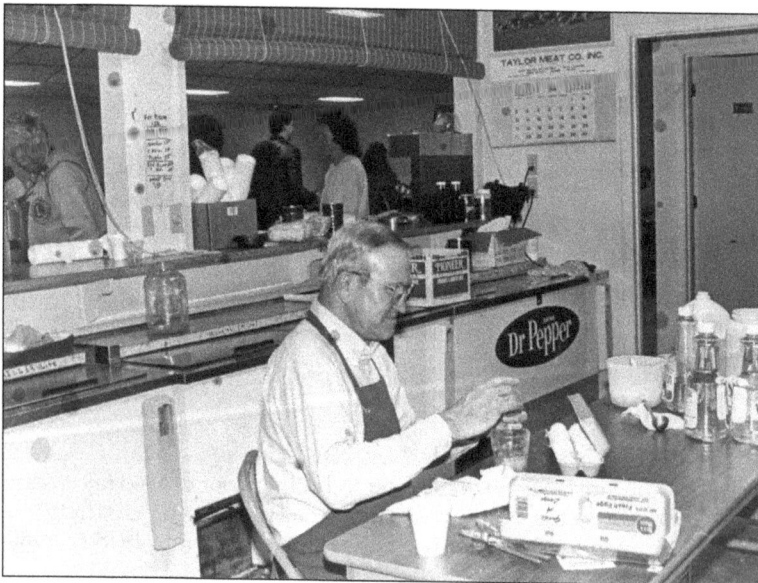

Marvin Sturm cracks eggs in preparation for the Hutto Lions Club Annual Pancake Supper on February 11, 1988, held in the Hutto Fire Hall. Notice Jerry Roznovak, Mike Sturm, and Ann Exley from left to right in the background. (Courtesy Sturm family collection.)

Jim Cage Sr. was a deacon of Little Ebenezer Baptist Church and was the first African American elected to the Hutto City Council, where he served for 12 years. On November 22, 1989, at age 61, Jim Cage Sr. became the 34th recipient of a heart transplant at the Central Texas Heart Institute of Seton Medical Center. Jim Cage Sr. died on February 7, 1997, having accomplished much for the Hutto community. (Courtesy Emma Kellough Collection.)

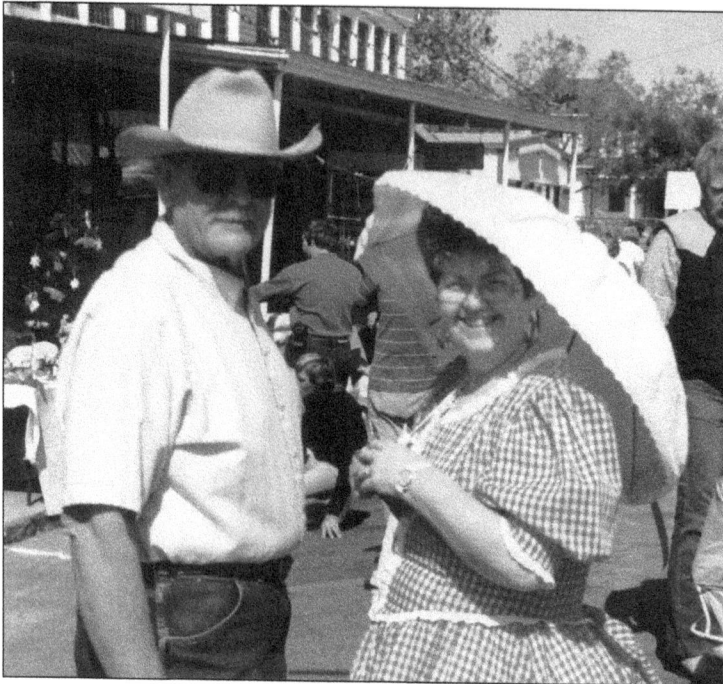

On October 21, 1989, Gus Leon Almquist and his wife, Peggy, celebrated the Hutto Olde Tyme Days. Gus Leon Almquist graduated from Hutto High School in 1950. Gus was one of many generations of Hutto farmers of Swedish background and also during his later years worked at the Hutto Independent School District. Gus and Peggy had four children—Greg, Glen, Gary, and Paula—all of whom graduated from Hutto High School. (Author's collection.)

Johanna (Olander) Wimberly is pictured in her traditional Swedish attire for the Santa Lucia celebration at Hutto Lutheran Church on December 10, 1989. Santa Lucia Day is a celebration of light in Sweden and is officially observed on December 13 each year. Notice the printed dala horses and flowers on her dress. The dala horse (in Swedish *Dalahäst*) is a traditional wooden statuette or depiction of a horse originating in the Swedish province of Dalarna. In the older days, the dala horse was mostly a toy for children; however, today it is a symbol of Sweden. (Author's collection.)

The Hutto Volunteer Fire Department poses in the 1990s with their new jaws of life equipment when the department was housed in what is now El Poblanito Mexican Restaurant at 301 West Street. Pictured from left to right are (first row) Frank Rendon, Danny Thiele, Ken Wahrmund, Kimball "Cajun" Foster, and John Corbett; (second row) Mrs. Danny Thiele, Linda Thiele, Doug Thiele, Richard Sweeney, unidentified, and Terry Thiele. (Courtesy Hutto Chamber of Commerce Collection.)

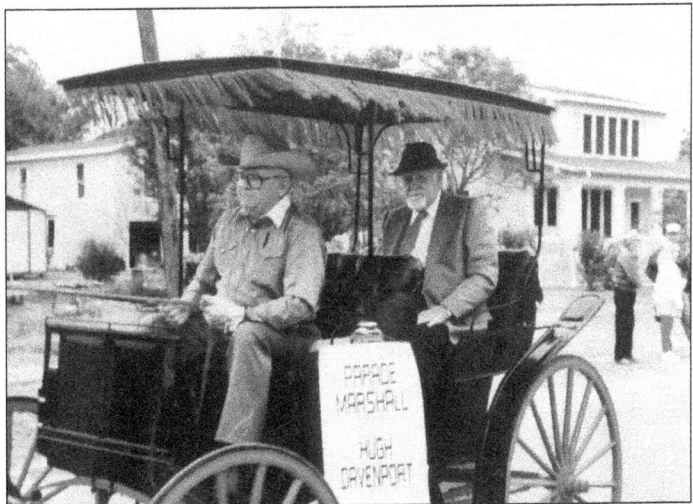

N. G. "Bunky" Whitlow, a Round Rock banker and icon with his antique horse-drawn surrey with the fringe on top, rides with Hugh S. Davenport Sr., a lifelong Hutto resident and former postmaster, in October 1992 on Farley Street. Hugh was honored as the 1992 Hutto Chamber of Commerce Grand Parade Marshal in the Hutto Olde Tyme Days Parade. (Courtesy Hugh S. Davenport Sr. Collection.)

The City of Hutto was once housed in the building originally built for Taylor Banc Savings at 102 East U.S. Highway 79. The building was a 1992 default purchase for $65,000 through the FDIC and later sold for $260,000 to Texas Pawn and Jewelry in 2004, with the proceeds earmarked to benefit the library. (Author's collection.)

Charlie and Clarice Hanstrom are icons of the Hutto community; both were selected Hutto Citizen of the Year—Charlie in 1990 and Clarice in 1993. Charlie was born on April 23, 1920, and ran the waterworks for 39 years and the sewer system for the City of Hutto for 22 years. Clarice was born on July 28, 1926, and they married on February 9, 1946. She worked in banking for most of her career, and both consistently gave back to the Hutto community. They have three grown children: Aleda Hannah, Marilyn Kay, and Charles Thomas. (Courtesy Charles and Clarice Hanstrom Collection.)

This is a postcard of Henrietta the Hippo, a 14,000-pound concrete hippopotamus statue, which has been a Hutto local and tourist attraction since purchased and placed on East Street by the Hutto Chamber of Commerce in 1982. Murray McDonald helped to arrange the purchase from Double D Statuary, and Josh Richards delivered Henrietta to Hutto, blowing out several trailer tires along the way. Thousands of these Hutto Chamber of Commerce postcards have been mailed and distributed throughout the world. (Courtesy Ron Whitfield Photography.)

Elgene "Buddy" Holmstrom of Hutto was honored by his induction into the Texas Amateur Athletic Foundation Hall of Fame in 1996. During his fast-pitch softball career from 1946 to 1982, he played in 9 world, 29 state of Texas, and 15 regional tournaments. He was named to the TAAF All-State Team for 15 years and was selected as Most Valuable Player in three of those tournaments. Buddy pitched in the longest game in Amateur Softball Association history, which was over five hours long and lasted 28 innings. In the 1962 season, he allowed only four earned runs with 261 strikeouts and had a .341 batting average. (Courtesy Buddy Holmstrom Collection.)

This photograph was taken from atop an East Street building of the crowd awaiting the parade on East and Farley Streets during Hutto Olde Tyme Days. The Hutto Chamber of Commerce was founded in 1986 and held the first Hutto Olde Tyme Days Celebration that same year. (Courtesy Hutto Chamber of Commerce Collection.)

The 1999 AA State Championship Hutto Lady Hippos volleyball team is the only team in the history of Hutto to win a state championship. Through hard work and dedication, this team compiled a season record of 34 wins and 6 losses. Pictured from left to right are (first row) Crystal Duffie (senior) No. 20, Shelley Padgett (senior) No. 12, Kara Wells (senior) No. 10, Emily Fowler (senior) No. 21, and Kimberly Francis (senior) No. 15; (second row) Megan O'Neal (junior) No. 13, Melissa Bonnet (junior) No. 24, Melissa Angell (sophomore) No. 25, Abbey Hester (junior) No. 23, and Stacy Stanley (junior) No. 14; (third row) Katie O'Neal (freshman) No. 31, Brandy Saul (sophomore) No. 32, Alisha Bateman (junior) No. 11, Molly Hester (sophomore) No. 22, and coach Lacy O'Shoney; (fourth row) team managers Jessica Hardi and Nikki Hester, head coach Janiece Nelson, and team manager Jenny Oris. (Courtesy Janiece Nelson.)

Hutto High School Hi-Steppers Drill Team and the Hutto High School Band behind them participate in the Hutto Olde Tyme Days on the parade route on Farley Street. This October 20, 2001, photograph shows the Hutto Chamber of Commerce building (the Hanstrom building) in the background to the right. (Courtesy Hutto Chamber of Commerce Collection.)

Lee "Shorty" Martinez is pictured with his wife, Gloria (Balderas) Martinez, at his retirement from the Hutto Co-op. Lee worked for the Hutto Co-op Gin for almost his entire adult life. Lee worked part-time beginning in 1951 and full-time from 1962 until the Hutto Co-op Gin permanently closed in 2003. During that time, Lee worked for the following general managers: H. E. Gainer, John Saul, Vincent Johnson, Marshall Ford, Victor Stern, William Albert, and Bill Stern. (Courtesy Rios family collection.)

Shown from left to right on February 26, 2006, are five of the past mayors of Hutto: Mike Fowler (2000–2004, with a total of 25 years of elected service to the City of Hutto), Carl Stern (1961–1970, also was a councilman and the chief financial officer for the City of Hutto, provided over 40 years of total service to the city), Ed Schmidt (1970–1990, longest serving mayor in the history of Hutto, also served nine years as a city councilman), Mike Ackerman (2004–2006), and Ken Love (2006–2009, the first black mayor of the City of Hutto). This picture was taken in the Hutto Lutheran Church fellowship hall following the dedication of the State of Texas Historical Marker for the Hutto Lutheran Cemetery. (Author's collection.)

Four

RAPID CHANGE AND GROWING FORWARD

This photograph taken by Ron Whitfield shows both the new and old water towers in Hutto prior to the old one being taken down. The smaller 90-feet-above-grade, orange and white, 26,000-gallon water tower was built by Charles Evald Hanstrom in 1910, when the water supply was privately owned. It was replaced in 1990 by a 140-feet-above-grade, more modern, 100,000-gallon water tower. (Author's collection.)

This 1995 photograph taken from the approximate location of the Hutto Chamber of Commerce shows the dirt removal and street work on East Street as part of a City of Hutto infrastructure improvement project. At that time, city hall was still located in the second building from the far end of the picture. Councilman Murray McDonald is shown with a construction worker at extreme left center. Murray McDonald and his wife, Joscelyn, own the third and fourth buildings up from U.S. Highway 79. (Courtesy Hutto Chamber of Commerce Collection.)

This 21st-century photograph taken from Front Street just south of the railroad tracks shows the most longtime iconic image of Hutto: the north-side historic buildings of East Street. The Hutto business center was originally located on the south side until a tornado destroyed many of the structures, and in the 1890s, most of the business activity was relocated to the north side of the railroad tracks. The cars for sale at the Hutto Autoplex clearly put the picture in this century. (Author's collection.)

The beautiful Klattenhoff House was originally built by Germany native William Klattenhoff (1855–1928), who immigrated to Texas in 1872 at age 17. His work on the International and Great Northern Railroad brought him to Hutto, where he purchased land in 1876. Much of this information is from the Texas Historical Commission marker dedicated in 2002. Earl Klattenhoff and his wife, Jan, have allowed their Hutto-area home, located off of FM 685, to be in two major motion pictures, *Flesh and Bone* and *Courage Under Fire*, as well as a music video and numerous national television commercials. (Courtesy Klattenhoff family collection.)

Leo Perez, Hutto Co-op Gin superintendent, throws the switch, shutting down the cotton gin for the final time in Hutto in 2001 and ending a long, hard, and wet harvesting and ginning season. According to Bill Stern, the Hutto Co-op Gin processed the last bale of cotton and was shut down at about 11:00 in the morning on October 17, 2001, ending an 60-year-plus era of agricultural prominence in Hutto. (Courtesy Vic and Bertha Stern family collection.)

Founders of Hippos Unlimited, from left to right, are Mike Fowler, Troy McMillin, Rose (Aguilar) McMillin, and John Stern at Hutto Olde Tyme Days in 2007. Hippos Unlimited is a 501(c)3 nonprofit organization that states its primary purpose as "to advertise and promote the Hutto community in a positive manner through the use of its primary identifier, the hippopotamus." (Author's collection.)

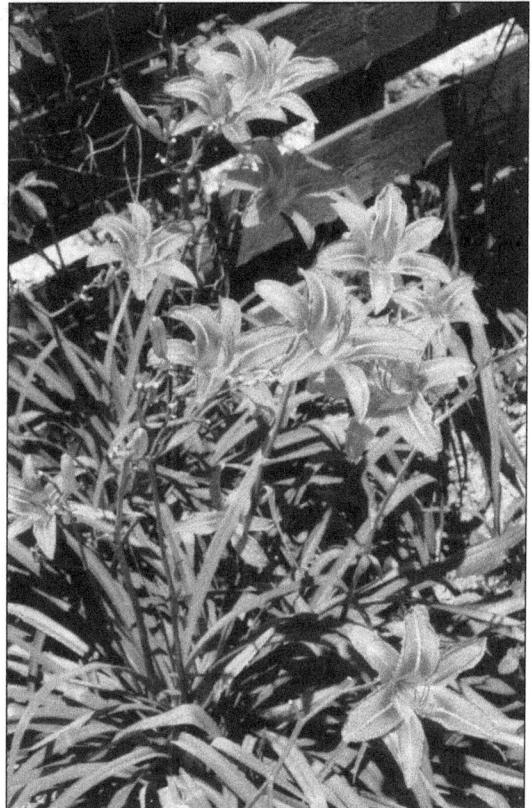

On February 5, 2009, the Hutto City Council, at the request of the Keep Hutto Beautiful Commission, adopted the orange crush daylily as the "Official Flower of the City of Hutto." The orange crush daylily is an excellent visual attraction that has a display of color with rich orange blooms and a rose-red eyezone that shows above deep blue-green foliage. This fragrant flower is stunning in a mass planting, has good performance, is easy to propagate through division or from seeds, and is well acclimated to the climate and soils of Hutto. (Author's collection.)

This is an aerial of Hutto before major development. Taken March 1999, it shows the old town area of Hutto surrounded by farmland. On the left at U.S. 79 and FM 685, the new Hutto High School is being built; five months later in August, the school was open for its first classes. The first graduating class for the new high school was in 2000. The only subdivisions apart from the 1911 incorporated area are the 1980s Cottonwood subdivision and the 1990s Clark's Crossing subdivision. State Highway 130 does not even appear in this photograph. (Author's collection.)

This 2009 aerial photograph looking in a southern direction shows, to the left, a portion of Hutto's old downtown area, what remains of the Co-op structures, and the pad work for the new Hutto Post Office. In the middle of the picture are the Nadine Johnson Elementary School and Hutto High School along with the Home Depot and Lowe's stores, which are also visible. To the right is the 91-mile State Highway 130 toll road, which stands out as it crosses U.S. Highway 79. The Hutto Economic Development Corporation (HEDC) is working to create economic positives for the Hutto community. There have been five presidents of HEDC and, while many served longer on the HEDC board, their terms as president were Ed Schmidt (1997–2000), Ron Whitfield (2000–2003), Tim Porter (2003–2005), Mahlon Arnett (2005–2006), and Mario Perez (2006–present). (Courtesy Hutto Economic Development Corporation.)

Visit us at
arcadiapublishing.com